SIX STEPS FROM
WIGAN PIER

In Memoriam Avril Fishwick

SIX STEPS FROM WIGAN PIER

*And a bag of Uncle Joe's
Mint Balls*

JOHN SHARROCK TAYLOR

Old Wigan Pier looking east towards the tower of the Trencherfield Mill

WIGAN PIER. 39.

First published 2016 by DB Publishing, an imprint of JMD Media Ltd,
Nottingham, United Kingdom.

ISBN 978-1-78091-543-2

CONTENTS

INTRODUCTION

What does Gandalf have in common with George Formby, Oliver Cromwell and a girl who sang for Hitler with military secrets hidden in her knickers? The answer, of course, is Wigan. Not long ago, over a pint of Sam Adams in a Minneapolis bar, my son Richard casually mentioned Frigyes Karinthy's *Six Degrees of Separation*, the theory that each one of us is no more than six 'steps' from any other person on the face of the planet. Initially sceptical, I soon realised that I'd stumbled upon a wonderful framework for one of my favourite activities: telling tales.

Wigan is a grand old town (the Romans knew it well). From the earliest times it has been a rich source of pies, tripe, cow-heels, coal, cotton, culture and, above all, stories. Some of the tales in this book connect with me or my family. All of them connect in some way with Wigan, and while a few start and finish within a cock-stride of the Pier, others will take us as far afield as Gallipoli, the Deep South of the United States during the civil rights struggles of the 1950s and the humid jungles of Central America in two bloody civil wars.

This is an utterly personal selection of topics, though when I first thought of it I had the vague idea that it ought to be more or less comprehensive. Neither sport nor Northern Soul are at all my scenes, but how could I write a Wigan book without the Warriors, the Latics or the Verve? Well, I managed the first two with the help of a fanatical brother but, having listened to a couple of tracks without being able to detect anything even vaguely resembling my idea of music, I realised that the third was far beyond my capabilities – though I have to assert that Wigan's Ovation, which featured my wife Val's cousins Pete and Phil Preston, actually played quite recognisable tunes. In any case, the idea of being able to encapsulate Wigan in a mere 65,000 words went right out of the window when I began to take a serious look at the truly enormous range of talent our town has produced.

How many degrees of separation are there between my wife's Aunt Winnie and Martin Luther King? Far fewer than you might have imagined.

CHAPTER 1

I WAS A BARMAN'S BOTTOM KNOCKER

The Incident of the Exploding Bus Driver was one of the more memorable moments during my occasional forays into the real world. And before we go into the whys and wherefores of the explosion, which happened one fine Summer morning in 1966 on the A49 near Eccleston, I'd better say something about that real world. In the bar the other night after choir practice, my friend Professor Jim Alty, former head of the Turing Institute and a professional ponderer on the nature of reality, spoke of the possible existence of parallel universes. The idea immediately rang a bell. I taught in schools for thirty-eight years and I would have retired a millionaire if I'd had a grand for every time somebody told me, 'You teachers don't know you're born. You should try living in the real world.'

I've never been quite sure about this 'real world' my various interlocutors believed they were living in and I wasn't. Perhaps they thought mine didn't contain such afflictions as mortgages, mothers-in-law, income tax, gas bills and in-growing toenails. Perhaps they were misled by the old nine-to-four cliché. If so, I would have been delighted to have them shadow me through my seven-day, seventy-odd-hour working week as a headmaster and even let them have a go at unravelling Wayne, the Year Ten psychopath, who would insert the chuck key on the invisible side in the hope that it would fly out and maim the CDT teacher when the bench drill was started up.

After twenty-four years of failing to locate reality in places as exotic as Whelley and Platt Bridge, Val and I decided to seek it farther afield. In 1991 we flew to New York with Richard (11) and Will (9), bought a van and drove a meandering four-thousand-mile route through the southern USA, Mexico and Guatemala to take up jobs in San Salvador. We climbed active volcanoes, became marginally involved in two civil wars, heard a lot of shooting and bombs going off and stared uncomfortably down the wrong end of some sub-machine guns. Nothing, we felt, could possibly be more real than this, and we came home after three years avid to tell our friends and family all about it. It turned out that they couldn't have cared less about our adventures in Central America (that was Kansas, wasn't it, where Dorothy's Uncle Henry made the Scarecrow?) but they were deeply worried about all the *Coronation Street* episodes we'd missed. It seemed that the elusive portal into the real world was located in some place called Wetherfield.

In spite of those missed episodes I've been something of a Corrie fan ever since that first gritty episode in 1960. And of course that word 'gritty' is the key to this whole reality business. When folk tell me I need to live in the real world they mean the world of real people who do real jobs such as mining, weaving and steel-making, except of course that hardly anybody in 'the West' does those jobs any more, though they were still doing some of them when I became a teacher in the 1960s. And that brings me a step or two nearer to the Exploding Bus Driver.

I wasn't the first schoolmaster to darken the family doorstep. That dubious honour belongs to my great, great, great grandfather Thomas Shaw, who was already busily dusting the seats of juvenile Wigan trousers by the time of the 1841 Census. But I'm fairly sure I was the first in our family to attend a university. The United States has a long tradition of youngsters working their way through college, and from the mid-20th century this gradually became the norm in Britain too. Student grants (those were the days!) made it unnecessary for most of us to take on weekday or weekend jobs but, together with most of my contemporaries, I did a variety of work during the vacations. Christmas mail delivery paid quite well (tips were much more plentiful in the working-class terraces than in the posh suburbs such as Orrell or Wigan Lane) but after stamping the same serial number on several thousand identical brass tags throughout an eight-hour shift in the aptly named Grimwood electrical elements factory in Skem, I cheerfully opted for a happier, if penniless, Easter.

My favourite forms of summer reality were bus conducting and working in the linoleum warehouse. The lino was made at Heapey near Chorley by a firm called Witters, and the Head Foreman, a very tall elderly chap called Eric who wore an enormous tweed cap, surprised me on my first day by quoting Wittgenstein. Huge rolls of linoleum six feet in diameter were delivered from the factory and it was the job of our crew, a mixture of regulars and summer casuals, to prepare it for sale by cutting it into retail sizes. Each of the big rolls had to be grasped by the top and tipped over on to a 'bogy', a stoutly-built, iron-wheeled truck about three feet by four. If you positioned your bogy correctly the roll descended neatly on to it and balanced, so you could wheel it to the cutting machine with little effort. If you got it wrong, the bogy flirted out from underneath the roll and struck your shins at about a million miles an hour.

The trade label of our brand of linoleum was *Balatum*, a word which seemed to me to conjure up the South Sea Islands of Gauguin and Somerset Maugham, complete with lazily smoking volcanoes and voluptuous maidens in grass skirts. Such imaginings added a pleasingly surreal dimension to the mundane world of floor covering manufacture, and an even stranger layer of unreality was creeping in. I was already in love with the splendid tunes and unlikely plots of grand opera, and a South Sea island, presided over by the High Priest of the Great God Balatum, seemed the perfect setting for a Bizet or Weber extravaganza. I mentioned my fantasy during tea break. To my surprise, the whole crew, including the regulars, seized on the idea, and the appearance of our philosophical foreman at the door of the cutting shop would be a cue for a muttered stage direction: 'Enter Eric, Master of the Rolls and High Priest of Balatum, in ceremonial cap.'

In the middle of the summer, when more people than usual were on holiday, there came a lull in the retail demand for lino, and we began to be afraid that some of us would be laid off. It was Danny, one of the regulars, a smiling leprechaun, who came up with a solution: 'Boys, I'm convinced there's something weird about one of them rolls in the warehouse. You know, that big black bugger in the far right-hand corner. I reckon if we was to sacrifice an apprentice or two to that big sod all our troubles would be over in a flash.'

The linoleum cutting machine was operated by three men: the Buttonman, the Barman and the Barman's Bottom Knocker. The Buttonman was in charge of the operation as a whole, starting and stopping the process and generally making sure that there was no unnecessary loss of lino, time or fingers. It was the Barman's job to load the roll on to the cutter and he did this by running a huge, gleaming

13

The jingle of phantom spurs   *William Scott/ Bigstock*

steel bar through the centre of it as it lay on the bogy, locating one of the sockets of the machine with the free end of the bar and then lifting the roll so the handle end could also be dropped into its respective socket. As the Barman's Bottom Knocker I had the most intriguing title, albeit the least interesting job. The blades on each side of the table were designed to give a neat trim to the edges of the finished length. Newly cut lino is sticky stuff, and the severed ribbon of material would still adhere to the roll, so it was my job to tap it gently with a wooden cloth yard so that it fell off into the waste basket. After a couple of weeks at this fascinating task I was promoted to Barman and that was where I almost came to grief.

After packaging and labelling, the retail rolls were scooped up at high speed by the Scammell men, so called from the trucks in which they dashed between the warehouse and various shipping terminals. The Scammell men were a completely different species from us. Tough Klingons to our puny Earthlings, they spoke only to each other, in monosyllabic Scammell grunts. They were on piece work, which meant that their earnings depended on the number of deliveries they were able to make in a day, so when they entered the warehouse they literally hit the ground running and dashed with their handcarts along the narrow passages between the big rolls, in the certain knowledge that they had absolute priority.

The concept of induction training was still far in the future, but on our first working day Eric had impressed on us that 'You must never, and I mean NEVER get in the way of a Scammell man.' But I didn't just get in the way of a Scammell man. I knocked him arse over tip and made him turn a somersault.

One afternoon, soon after my apotheosis into the mysteries of barmanship, I was trundling my bogy along a side alley of the warehouse, the steel bar of the cutting machine already transfixing the roll I was carrying and sticking out a good three feet ahead of it. This, of course, would have been strictly contrary to elf-and-safety had such a notion then existed. I wasn't looking where I was going. In fact, I was quietly composing a philosophical aria for Eric, basso cantante (*Ludwig, mein Freund, wo ist Dein Tractatus?*). I emerged from my side alley into the main thoroughfare at the precise moment Kevin the Scammell man reached the junction. There was no possibility of avoiding a collision. Kevin's handcart struck the projecting steel pole and stopped dead. Kevin did not stop dead. He described a less-than-graceful arabesque over the top of the pole and landed with a crash on the concrete floor. Struggling into a sitting position he glared at me across the overturned handcart.

'I'm truly sorry,' I began penitently, 'I do hope you're not hurt.'

Kevin neither swore nor raised his voice, which only added to the menace of his reply: 'I'm the one who's sorry. I'm sorry I've not time to give you the kicking you deserve. Not now, anyway, because my team's due at the docks in less than an hour. But tomorrow's my afternoon off and I'll be waiting when you come off shift.'

I'm not tall and Kevin wasn't much bigger than me but he was clearly tough, determined and a lot fitter than any effete student opera buff. Two or three years older than me, dark-haired and a lot better looking, he reminded me of James Dean, and I definitely didn't fancy my chances in what Jimmy's *On the Waterfront* character would no doubt have called a 'rumble'. Even so, I was enjoying my time at Witters, the money was good, and I had no intention of being bullied out of the job. Calling in sick on the following day would merely have postponed matters, so I decided with great misgivings to tough it out.

As he had promised, Kevin was waiting a hundred yards from the works gates when I came off shift the following afternoon. News of impending disaster travels fast, and a small crowd had gathered to witness my death. We faced each other like gunfighters along the length of a silent western street, and as I slowly began to walk towards my adversary I swear I could hear the jingle of phantom spurs.

Kevin was clad in a rock star uniform of black leather jacket, jeans and motorcycle boots and I felt distinctly underdressed in my dungarees. With no more than ten yards between us we stopped as if by mutual consent. In the Old West this would have been time to draw, so I reached into the bib pocket of my overalls and produced the rusty three-pound hammer we used for breaking up coke in the wash house at home. Kevin regarded me levelly from under dark eyebrows.

'Do you want a fight?'

'I'd rather have a pint.'

'Me too.'

As we settled in behind the long, scrubbed table in the Bull's Head, Danny muttered 'Jaysus, Jack, that was one stupendous bluff. I thought you wuz a gonner there my lad.'

'Bollocks!' The speaker was Dave, another of the Scammell crew. 'Kev was the one who was bluffing. After shooting his mouth off yesterday he had to come today, and he was praying you'd not turn up. Anyway, Ingrid, his girlfriend, wouldn't let him fight even if he wanted to.'

Kevin caught my eye across the table. 'She's scared I'd my spoil my good looks,' he said with a sheepish grin.

I was relieved that Kevin and I had managed to avoid the expected explosion but the same could not be said of my next foray into the real world, which happened the following summer when I did a stint on the Ribble buses. In those civilised days, buses had conductors. The driver's job was reckoned to be stressful enough without his having to collect the tuppences in addition to avoiding the cyclists, though nowadays he does all three, sometimes with tragic results. On the buses of my youth, the same driver and conductor normally acted as a team, but as relief conductors during the holiday period we students worked with a variety of mates.

My favourite two drivers were Jock and Vincent and they couldn't have been more different, though they both treated me cordially, shared their thick sandwiches and bought me pint mugs of tea that was even thicker than the butties. Jock was Glaswegian and spoke a breakneck variety of Scots which was fortunately impenetrable, because it included very many expletives. Vincent, a calm, gentle, softly-spoken young Catholic paterfamilias, only ever swore once in my hearing, but to great effect.

The last bus from Wigan to St Helens, on a Saturday night, crowded with drunken clubbers, was never any crew's favourite, and the whole of our shift had been particularly trying. No less than three previous buses had broken down under us and had to be towed away, to the annoyance of the stroppier passengers, who of course took it out on the hapless crew. And now, on the thinly populated stretch of road between Orrell Moor and Billinge, it looked as if mutiny was about to break out.

'What wilt tha do, lad, if we all get agate smashin' thi buzz up?' asked one reveller with an unpleasant leer.

I adopted a quarterdeck stance and the tone of Captain Bligh informing Mr Christian that a keelhauling was high on the agenda: 'Well, the Ribble Transport training manual says "Take off the ticket machine, attach it firmly to the forearm with the leather strap and beat the delinquent over the head with it." Your choice.'

'Nay, nay, lad. Ah wuz only jokin'.'

'Ahm not jokin'!' interjected a strident female voice. 'From Orrell Post to Billinge Lower Rant it's only fivepence ha'penny and you've charged me a tanner.'

'Sorry. Just give me a couple of minutes to finish collecting the fares and I'll give you your change.'

'You'll do no such thing. I want my ha'penny and I want it now.'

'Please be patient and I'll be with you in a second.'

'Patient? Patient, he sez! Will I heckerslike! I want my ha'penny. I've met your sort before. A ha'penny here, a ha'penny there and you'll be making a pretty penny on th' side.'

I raised my voice to a pitch suitable for hailing the maintop in a hurricane: 'Does anybody apart from this "lady" want to get off at Billinge Lower Rant? No? Good, because we're not stopping there.'

I didn't have time to put my threat into action because it was at this point that our ninety-seven horsepower diesel chose, with an almighty bang, to throw a connecting rod through the side of the engine block. In silence we rolled to an ignominious halt, trailing streamers of hot oil across the tarmac. Then Vincent spoke, more in sorrow than in anger and with perfect diction:

'That's th' fourth fucking bus that's gone tits up this shift.'

It wasn't in Vincent's nature to explode and it's fortunate that when Jock detonated a few days later nobody but I understood what he said, because there would certainly have been complaints and possibly sackings. It was that rare kind of British summer day when the temperature has already climbed into the eighties by mid-morning. We were trundling sedately along the A49 towards Eccleston with a chattering cargo of pleasantly buxom farmers' wives. Jock, thoroughly at peace with the world, was controlling the steering wheel with one hand and working greedily with the other to extract the last few puffs from his current Woodbine. Finally, realising that there were no more carcinogens to be savoured, he dropped the dog-end on the steel floor of the cab. Unfortunately, some careless mechanic back at the depot had left a wad of oil-soaked cotton waste in exactly the right spot to cause the most trouble. The hot day had vaporised the oil and as soon as Jock dropped his fag there was a whoosh and a sheet of flame which bade fair to fry him where he sat.

Jock slammed on the brakes and leapt clear. Quickly realising that the flammable vapour had exhausted itself, he reached back into the cab and grabbed the fire extinguisher, with the idea of soaking the smouldering remnants of cotton waste and making all safe. The extinguisher turned out to be a dud but fortunately there was another Ribble bus coming in the opposite direction, carrying both a serviceable extinguisher and a deeply disapproving inspector, who soon put paid to the remains of our fire and gave Jock a hearty rollocking for smoking on duty. Now the only thing still smouldering was Jock's temper, as he drove on in silence towards Eccleston, sitting in a pool of foam. Two minutes later, our extinguisher, which had sullenly refused to function when needed, exploded down the back of his neck.

Dandling Gandalf

'Of course I'm proud of Ian. We all are. And I couldn't care less whether he's *gay* or *straight*. But why does he have to keep going on about it all the time? If I had him here I wouldn't half give him a piece of my mind. You and Val don't insist on telling everybody you meet what you get up to behind your bedroom door, thank God. Those things are private, or should be.'

Joan Bamford OBE had taught generations of Wigan children to play the piano, including a little lad called Ian McKellen. A spare, erect, grey-haired septuagenarian, Joan could easily have been taken for the kind of vinegary spinster who was capable of disapproving of the whole of the 20th century, let alone the sexual shenanigans of theatrical knights, if there had not so often been a faint smile hovering around the corners of those thin lips.

Ian Murray McKellen was born in Burnley in 1939, but his parents, Denis and Margery, soon moved to Wigan with Ian and his sister Jean when Denis was appointed as Borough Engineer. Of his first experience of live theatre (*Peter Pan* at the Manchester Opera House, at the age of three) Ian records that he 'wasn't overly impressed. For one thing it wasn't a real crocodile and I could see the wires.' At nine, his parents' Christmas present was a toy Victorian theatre with movable characters.

The McKellens and the Bamfords were Congregationalists like Val's mother's family, the Fairhursts, and the 'congs' were then, and still are,

Jorge Restrepho

19

deeply involved in the Wigan arts scene. Denis McKellen was a lay preacher, an activity which calls on the same skills as acting, and Val's Aunt Winnie, whom you will meet again later in this book, recalled him as ever ready to declaim a Shakespearean soliloquy.

'Do you remember Ian?' I asked her.

'Of course I do. I dandled him on my knee when he was a baby.'

Ian acknowledges his sister Jean as a major influence. Five years older than Ian, she took him to his first Shakespeare productions, *Twelfth Night* and *Macbeth* at the Wigan Little Theatre, and he saw her play Bottom in a Wigan High School for Girls production of *A Midsummer Night's Dream*. The rest, as the cliché goes, is history and I have no intention of regurgitating the Stratford triumphs, the Oscar, BAFTA and Emmy nominations, the six Oliviers, the knighthood and the Tolkien wizardry. You know it all as well as I do, and probably better, for the man is one of the all-time greats. Curiously, one of his regrets is having dropped his Lancashire accent. Like him, I quite consciously abandoned mine, but we may both retain some echoes because not long ago someone told me I sounded like Ian McKellen. 'Well, we went to the same school,' I simpered, feeling absurdly flattered.

In fact, the McKellens moved to Bolton when Ian was twelve and I was five, so the Wigan Grammar School connection is tenuous. As I was later to do, the English staff at Bolton School ran yearly trips to the Royal Shakespeare Theatre and one of Ian's reminiscences rings a rather guilty bell:

'Each summer, I went on the school camp, pitched near Stratford-upon-Avon, where we saw the productions season after season. We queued through the night for half-a-crown-standing, wore ourselves out punting all day and we snoozed through stretches of the most eminent performances.'

I have to confess that after a very heavy night I too slumbered through parts of a Stratford play. It was Trevor Nunn's highly acclaimed production of *Romeo and Juliet*, starring Francesca Annis and, I blush to admit it, Ian McKellen.

Ian read English at St Catharine's College, Cambridge where he acted in Shakespeare's *Henry IV* opposite Derek Jacobi, for whom, he says, he had 'a passion that was undeclared and unrequited.' Fifty years on, they played two old queens in the TV series *Wicked*. It was dire. Kenny Williams and Larry Grayson would have done it so much better.

Ian publicly came out of the closet in a BBC Radio 4 programme, while discussing Margaret Thatcher's Section 28 legislation, which would criminalise 'the public promotion of homosexuality'. He has been active in the gay rights movement ever since. 'I immediately felt better in every way. I felt relieved that I wasn't lying. You know, when I was growing up in England, there were no gay clubs that I knew about. There were no bars. Homosexuals were shamed publicly and imprisoned. You were on your own, looking over your shoulder all the time.'

Well, I can certainly empathise with that, though I also understand Joan Bamford's irritation, less with her former pupil's emphatically public stance on gay rights, than with the flippant manner in which it is sometimes expressed. Not long ago Ian was advised by the Foreign Office not to go to Russia because of its laws against homosexuality.

'They couldn't protect me from those laws. Two and a half hours from London! In the land of Tchaikovsky, Diaghilev and Rudolf Nureyev, gay artists whose sexuality informed their work!' This is a man who famously went on a talk show in straight-laced Singapore, another country with strict anti-homosexuality laws, and asked the host 'Can you recommend any decent gay bars?'

Homophobia is a silly word for a silly phenomenon. 'Phobia' means 'fear'. Some lads have fancied each other from time immemorial, and though it can seem a bit odd for those of us who only fancy lasses, there's certainly nothing scary about it. I'm not even going to waste words and energy trying to convince you that some of my friends are gay, though of course some of them are. I'm wary of that patronising and frequently misused word 'tolerance' or I might be tempted to tell you that I grew up in a tolerant household, which would be an outrageous lie. My parents Bill and Beatrice were emphatically intolerant of a vast range of things, including each other, but homosexuality wasn't one of them. Norman, our next-door neighbour, was flamboyantly camp and his ceaseless flow of Wigan wit made us ache with laughter. Bill's idea of a good night out was six pints of mild in the Hare and Hounds, a back street boozer a friend of mine once described as being like 'Hell on a wet Christmas Eve', so Beatrice and Norman would trip off to dance and dine and

21

leave my father happily absorbed in his darts and dominoes.

I was amused at Ian McKellen's tart response to Damian Lewis's comment that *he* didn't want to end up as a slightly over-the-top fruity old actor condemned to a life of playing wizards: 'No one needs to feel sorry for me or Michael Gambon, or anyone else who has fallen victim to success.' He added slyly, 'I often get mistaken for Dumbledore. One wizard is very much like another… but I've had enough of being a gay icon and I've had enough of all this hard work, because, since I came out, I keep getting all these parts, and my career's taken off. I want a quiet life. I'm going back into the closet.'

As yet another fruity old wizard might put it, 'I don't believe it!'

CHAPTER 2

UP FOR TH' CUP

I may just possibly be the most un-sporty person on the face of this planet. There are probably cod and mackerel swimming around in the Irish Sea that can catch a ball better than I can. My almost total lack of athletic ability is puzzling, because both my parents were talented sportspersons who were utterly baffled by my fumbling efforts on the cricket and football fields. My mother Beatrice was a famous local swimmer, winning cups, shields and medals galore, and she later taught generations of Wigan girls at the public baths in Millgate, where my great uncle Jack Cockrell was superintendent. My dad Bill, a good footballer who coached the Highfield team, even continued to play the occasional match for them until after he turned fifty. On BBC radio

the day Stanley Matthews died, the interviewer quizzed his arch-rival:

'Mr Banks, some people reckoned Matthews was afraid of you.'

'Stan frightened of me? I couldn't even *catch* the bugger. I'd see them little bandy legs dribblin' towards me and I'd think "Oh 'ell, 'ere we go again."'

My mate John Aspinall, who also turned out for Highfield, said something similar about my dad's evasive skills, but Bill typically shrugged it off with: 'I've no option but play dodgems with 'em. If one of them big eighteen-year-olds charged me full on I'd fall to bits.'

Jim Sullivan, Wales & Wigan

23

It was at the Blue Coat School that I discovered how useless I was at the things my parents held dear. Anything involving physical co-ordination, from country dancing to gym, was a nightmare. It was not that I despised these activities. I simply couldn't do them. I tried, but my feet always seemed to get in the way. When we did PE I gazed with awe at Joan Barrow's apparently double-jointed ability to contort herself into any shape she chose, but both forward and backward rolls were, and remained, quite beyond me. I even joined in the lunchtime scratch games of football and cricket, but for obvious reasons was always the last to be picked for teams. During a school match, on the Rectory field, I attempted bowling at Tony Settle's wicket. By some fluke, my first ball was dead on, and Tony, who was gripping the bat the wrong way, ended up with bloody fingers. My second ball, a full toss, hit him straight between the eyes and raised a bump the size of a pigeon's egg. This was the end of my school cricketing career (and probably Tony's too) though I continued to be cannon fodder in our scratch matches on the vacant lot close to home, where my batting average could have stocked a whole poultry farm of ducks. Tony, incidentally, later became a very good countertenor but I swear my bowling had nothing to do with that.

I was only slightly better at rugby. I had looked askance at all those big boots but my dad said the way to avoid being kicked was to be brave and tackle low. I tried it and it worked. My victim was three times my age and twice my weight but he came down with a crash right on top of me. When I emerged from my daze, he was cradling me tenderly with a look of infinite concern, so one way or another I knew I'd stopped him. I did eventually more or less learn the rules of the game and was even able to explain some of them to my son Richard's Minnesotan brother-in-law, when we attended a Doncaster–Bedford rugby union match a couple of years ago, slyly adding that rugby is a bit like American football, but faster, more fearless and with a lot more blood. I suppose it's lumbering about in all that armour that makes the Yanks need a commercial rest break every five minutes but to me it's every bit as exciting as golf.

I suspect that part of my problem may be that I don't actually want sport to be exciting. Any match for me becomes much more bearable if it is combined with a sunny afternoon, a deckchair and a steady supply of anaesthetic, Theakston's for choice. The notable exceptions were those times when our sons played rugby for their school and Val and I bounced excitedly up and down on the bleachers screaming clueless encouragement. It seems that these things can skip generations and our lads have inherited not only their grandparents' strange fascination for mud, blood and pain, but also their mother's superb hand-eye co-ordination which, long before surgery dealt with her myopia, allowed her to clout rounders balls long distances with astounding accuracy. Rounders, of course, being a sport big hairy Americans call baseball, to disguise the fact that it's really a lasses' game.

When I was in short pants the great Joe Egan was still coaching Wigan Rugby, and although I never saw him play, for he retired in February 1946, five months before I was born, I came to know the legendary Jimmy Sullivan, who was not only part-owner of a garage near my home but also a friend and close neighbour of my future parents-in-law. By this time Mr Sullivan was partially incapacitated by a stroke but gained the admiration of all who knew him by his determination not to succumb to his physical limitations. With the left handle of the garden shears strapped to his body he could do a neater hedge-trimming job than most of us managed with two fully functioning hands.

Though I rubbed shoulders with this giant of the sport I never became a really enthusiastic spectator at Central Park or anywhere else, the notable exceptions being the two finals my family attended at Wembley in the late 1950s, where I felt fiercely partisan in support of my home town. Typically, I remember nothing of the matches themselves but a couple of the extraneous details are as clear as day. We didn't acquire our first family car until 1960, so we travelled to the 1959 final in an immaculate 1952 green Ford Zephyr loaned by a friend. The motorway era was still in the future, so a route had to be figured out. I was thirteen and Bill handed me the road atlas and AA book and told me to get on with it. I not only planned the route but memorised it, and fragments of it – Ackocks Green-Solihull-Knowle-Hatton – are lodged in my memory to this day.

On a long journey my father liked to leave home in the dark and drive into the dawn, a phrase I still find strangely romantic. We made unexpectedly good time and somewhere near St Albans Bill pulled off the road into a lay-by to catch up on some sleep before entering the City. We didn't need an alarm call because, almost exactly two hours later, the ten-ton lorry parked just ahead of us reversed into the Zephyr with an almighty crash. I clearly remember the surprisingly restrained dressing-down Bill gave to the trucker, not on the theme of his general carelessness but on the real possibility that my brother Stephen or I might have been between the truck and the car when the impact occurred.

The previous year, returning on the train from overcoming Workington, I had composed a victory song which received an enthusiastic reception from what I suppose must have been one of my earliest audiences. Fortunately for the annals of literature I don't remember any of it, but there is a Mike Harding ditty that some Wigan bard adapted as follows:

> *We are Wigan Rugby Club,*
> *The best in all the land,*
> *Marching on to Wemb-er-ley,*
> *And singing with the band.*
> *At home we are unbeatable,*
> *Away we are supreme,*
> *So give us a cheer, the lads are here,*
> *The Wigan rugby team.*
>
> *Although the game is tough and hard,*
> *The fans are good as gold,*
> *A happy family atmosphere*
> *Alike for young and old,*
> *So come on down and join us,*
> *Within our famous walls.*
> *We're more well-known than Wigan Pier*
> *Or Uncle Joe's Mint Balls.*

The 'good as gold' tag is a bit misleading. Some old codger was reckoned to have buttonholed John Monie, Wigan's great Australian coach, within a few days of his appointment and told him, 'We don't care about anybody else, lad, just make bloody sure tha beats Sentellins.'

The Wigan versus St Helens epic is one to rival Greece and Troy: four Wembley meetings, plus one Challenge Cup final at Murrayfield in Edinburgh and one at the Millennium Stadium in Cardiff when Wembley was closed for rebuilding. Three wins each – the first two at Wembley won by Saints, one of them in very controversial circumstances, and the next two by Wigan, including a 27-0 hammering in which, as my brother laconically puts it, 'Saints were lucky to get the nil'. Wigan won unexpectedly in Edinburgh in 2002 when Saints were clear favourites, but were soundly beaten two years later in Cardiff.

The 1966 St Helens win still rankles. Wigan had sold veteran hooker Bill Sayer – slow in the loose, but an ace scrummager – to Saints the year before. His replacement, Colin Clarke, had managed to get himself suspended, so a young prop forward called Tom Woosey stood in for the final. Woosey actually won the first scrum, to a mighty roar from the Wigan crowd, but hardly managed another throughout the afternoon. Alex Murphy, the wily St Helens international scrum-half, knew that his team mate Sayer could monopolise the scrums, so he repeatedly stood offside, conceding a stream of penalties, leading to scrums which St Helens invariably won, tiring the Wigan players out with constant tackling. Murphy's gamesmanship later prompted a rule change eliminating rewards for such deliberate infringements, but Alex had his cup winner's medal and couldn't have cared less. Though acknowledging that he was a fine player, my father despised him as 'Second-Man-in-Murphy', a cheap shot merchant who didn't fancy it much one on one, but liked to dish it out to opponents already held in a tackle. Murphy later became a highly controversial Wigan coach, some regarding him as a motivator and others as a dinosaur. In those days all the players were part-time and it was rumoured that Murphy would begin evening training with a tracksuit over his day clothes, then disappear to the dog track as soon as any directors were safely out of the way. He was allegedly sacked after pitching a telephone at vice-chairman Maurice Lindsay during a discussion over bonus payments.

During all of my childhood, Wigan Athletic played second fiddle to the much more famous Cherry-and-Whites, though they had their moments. One of these occurred at St James's Park in January 1954, when as humble members of the Lancashire Combination they were drawn to face Newcastle United away in the third round of the Cup. The Geordies were at the time one of the most powerful teams in England, boasting a number of internationals, headed by the legendary Jackie Milburn. Jack Livesey put the Latics 2-1 up deep into the second half, only for Milburn to equalise with a brilliant solo goal, and the game ended in a highly improbable 2-2 draw.

In those days there were no floodlights at Springfield Park, so the replay was held on a midweek afternoon, with the future Latics chairman Dave Whelan playing the trombone in the brass band that provided the pre-match entertainment. Wigan's stand had burned down the previous year, the new stand was still under construction, and Newcastle's chairman loftily courted controversy by refusing to allow his players to use the rudimentary temporary changing facilities at the Wigan ground. They changed at the public baths in Millgate and travelled to the ground in their kit. Latics were quickly 0-2 down but fought back strongly as Billy Lomax scored to make it 1-2. Then every eye in the crowd saw Newcastle's goalkeeper Simpson step back over the line as he caught a powerful shot from Jackie Lyon. Unfortunately, both the referee and linesman were graduates of the Blind School and this time there was to be no fairy-tale ending.

There have been two *anni mirabili* when both the Warriors and the Latics won at Wembley in the same year. In 1985 the Cherry-and-Whites beat Hull 28-24 in what many regard as the best cup final ever played. In a nice colemanball, BBC commentator Ray French berated Wigan for poor tactics only seconds before grinning winger Henderson Gill touched down for a splendid solo try. A couple of weeks later, on the same pitch, the Latics easily won the Freight Rover Trophy by overcoming Brentford by three goals to nil.

During the past few years the Latics' reputation as giant-killers has been sealed by a couple of stupendous victories over an internationally renowned team assembled with perhaps half a billion pounds of Abu Dhabi oil money. Their defeat of Manchester City, hailed in the press as possible winners of all four main trophies, would have seemed triumph enough if Wigan had not *already* vanquished City to win the previous year's FA Cup. It was neither lucky nor undeserved. On the day, the

Latics simply outplayed their nominally far superior opponents. The rugby team then went on to beat Hull at Wembley and complete a double of its own by polishing off Warrington in a lively encounter at Old Trafford.

Even in the mid-1960s, Springfield Park still had no floodlights, so the FA Cup replay against Football League Doncaster Rovers had to be held on a weekday afternoon. Wigan Grammar School Headmaster George Merriman had issued an edict that anyone sloping off to the match would be severely dealt with, though it was rumoured that at least one member of staff had decided to risk it and several lads certainly did. Score updates arrived by clandestine runner throughout the afternoon and the news that the Latics had gone 1-0 up early in the second half produced a surreptitious cheer which permeated steadily through the school. It finished 3-1 to Wigan, the man of the match being the Latics' legendary centre-forward Harry Lyon who had been carried off on a stretcher early in the piece with an ankle injury, only to return, allegedly fortified with a double whisky, to bang in a hat-trick. Compare that with some of today's overpaid prima donnas rolling around on the turf in imaginary agony. They don't make them like Harry any more.

Christmas In Delhi

From *No Baboons in India* by John Sharrock Taylor

Friends and family in Europe and the Americas are sending us tales of their first snows, and the weather here in northern India is decidedly parky. According to a colleague there are a hundred thousand monkeys in the greater Delhi area. All I can say is that if this includes any brass ones they are at serious risk. The charts show that December and January are always chilly, influenced as they are by the icy breath of the Himalayas, but we find ourselves in the midst of an early cold snap with temperatures hovering just above freezing.

Northern India builds its houses with the forty-degree heat of summer in mind. Ceilings are high, walls un-insulated and doors and windows left with howling gaps. We go to an office scarcely warmed by its two token fan heaters, in as many layers of clothing as possible, including gloves, scarves and hats. The woollies stay on throughout the day and as I sit at my desk I wear my fleece round my waist, like a Masonic apron, to protect my nether regions from the draughts. Going to the loo is an operation which has to be thought out in advance.

The men and women working on the building site are hardier. They emerge from their tents and improvised shelters and strip off most of their clothing in the bleak dawn to wash in the near-freezing jets from hosepipes. Much of the time the countryside is fogbound and we drive to the campus through villages where people

A Christmas Carol
Neftali/ Bigstock

Monkey in the Mist   *Mino/ Bigstock*

muffled up to the eyes in thick shawls huddle round cow dung fires, and camels and buffaloes loom mysteriously for a moment before disappearing again into the fog. Peafowl warily roost on roofs to avoid the dogs which try to sneak up under cover of the mist.

As usual we are into a busy round of end-of-year events, including my Indian version of *A Christmas Carol* presented by the boarders. Dickens was a storytelling genius and the archetypical appeal of the repentant Ebenezer Patel across time, continents and cultures is truly moving.

In spite of the weekly three-hour round trip to and from the city through the terrifying Delhi traffic I have enjoyed directing the choir for the British community carol service, accompanied on the piano by an impressively talented and surprisingly humble and co-operative High Commissioner. Val has nervously overseen a primary school nativity play with a lively cast of thousands of Giles children of all shapes and sizes. Nervously, because Hari, our wildly enthusiastic Hindu drama teacher, has managed to sneak episodes about Moses and the Bulrushes and the Sermon on the Mount into the more usual narrative of Mary, Joseph and the baby Jesus.

The cold weather has arrived just in time for the High Commissioner's Christmas garden party and we have never seen anything quite like it. The tropical gardens of the embassy have been blanketed with polystyrene snow, and concealed blue spotlights add to the illusion of a freezing English winter evening. Small white lights twinkle frostily in the jacaranda and flame-of-the-forest-trees. Muffled up in overcoats, brightly coloured scarves and bobble hats, we eat figgy pudding, drink mulled wine and sing carols. In the opening solo of 'In the Bleak Midwinter', Val's light soprano is as pure and steady as when I first heard it in a Lancashire carol service forty years ago.

CHAPTER 3

THE LAND OF THE JEWEL

In 1991, Val and I sold most of our possessions apart from what we could cram into two suitcases and a couple of plywood tea chests. Then we flew to the USA, bought a big Chrysler van, and embarked with our sons Richard (11) and Will (9) on a meandering four-thousand-mile route from Connecticut through the southern states of the USA, Mexico and Guatemala, to El Salvador, where we were to take up posts in the British school in the capital. The ancient Mayan name for El Salvador is Cuscatlán, the Land of the Jewel.

To plunge into Mexico across the international bridge over the Rio Grande is to move instantaneously into a different world. To the north are Disney and the realms of corporate enterprise, flashing neon, plastic food, social security and excess; to the south, riches and squalor, desert and selva, volcano, Aztec temple, glacier and Tierra del Fuego, occasionally displaying the panoply of King Burger and Queen Dairy

The Land of the Jewel

but often just making do, as different from the north as enchiladas are from fish and chips.

Once out of the terminal at Nuevo Laredo, the road to Saltillo and Monterrey threads through semi-desert between high barren sierras. Traffic is heavy: staggering, high-piled 1950s-style pantechnicons with flapping tarpaulins vie with battered pickups and minibuses, held together by rust and prayer, crammed with people and trussed live fowls. The poorest kind of market stalls crowd the roadside. At every crossroads and traffic light, traders leap forward with sweets and souvenirs, while children offer to smear the windscreen in return for a few centavos. The struggling villages have names like San Juan Sin Agua (St John Without Water) and, wistfully, Más Mañana (More Tomorrow). The absence of hard shoulders is unnerving. The surface of this main trunk highway is reasonable, about as good as a poor B-road at home, but a few inches to the right are ruts, rocks and murderous cactus scrub. The road rises and falls over a spur of the sierra in a series of hairpin loops. On each blind bend the 'artics' strain to overtake each other, often chugging abreast for a quarter of a mile and completely blocking the highway in both directions.

A friend had warned us not to drive at night on Guatemalan roads because burros never carried tail lights and truck drivers whose vehicles had broken down left them unlit and protected only by branches and boulders strewn on the roadway behind. We arrived late at the border crossing. The transit formalities for the van were protracted, and while the Mexican official typed with one finger on an ancient Remington I whiled away the time by flirting with his pretty eight-year-old daughter. Finally, all was done. The official rummaged in the tray of odds and ends on his desk and then called to his colleagues: 'Quién tiene la llave?'

'What key?' we wondered impatiently. It turned out to be the key to the huge padlock securing the heavy chain spanning the road into Guatemala. After much muttering and fiddling in drawers and pockets, the key was finally produced and we were free to go. It was already dusk, but we were not unduly worried. Dan Sanborn's guide, which had seldom failed us, indicated that there was a good hotel only a couple of miles across the frontier. We reached it and I have never met with such utterly uncharacteristic indifference in any hotel, restaurant or public place in twenty-odd years' experience of Spain and Latin America. The young female receptionist was elegant and unsmiling.

'Good evening, do you have a double room for tonight?'

'No.'

'A single?'

'No. The hotel is full.'

'My wife and I have two young children with us and we are concerned about travelling these unlit roads at night. Could we perhaps sleep in our van in the grounds of the hotel?'

'No.'

'Then can you direct us to an alternative hotel or guest house?'

'No.'

Now, with more than a quarter of a century of Spanish at my disposal, I would be more than capable of wiping the floor with such a glacial adversary, while pressing all the cultural buttons necessary to make managers and assistant managers run around in all directions. Then, my only recourse was silent rage.

Seething with frustration and fury I follow the headlights' track along the tunnel of the now pitch-dark and deserted road. I am keyed-up to fever pitch with responsibility and guilt. Val is quietly anxious, but the children, mercifully, have fallen asleep in the rear seat. We go on for miles with hardly a sign of human habitation. Suddenly a lamp is flashed in the darkness ahead. I brake as a soldier steps into the path of the van. He is one of a patrol of perhaps a dozen. I note the forage caps, the camouflage fatigues, the levelled sub-machine gun, the young lieutenant, immaculate and stern in his polished jackboots.

'Are you mad? Nobody should be driving at night in this country. Don't you know there is a civil war on? Where have you come from?'

'Mexico… the United States of America… England.'

'Where are you headed?'

'El Salvador.'

Eyebrows are raised and meaningful looks exchanged.

'Another dangerous country. Even worse than this one.'

The lieutenant peers into the back of the van and sees the sleeping children: 'Listen, you are very fortunate that we found you. Guerrillas have blown up the road bridge just ahead of you. Our people have put in a temporary structure. You will need to drive dead slow. The sergeant here will walk in front of you with his lantern. And seven kilometres beyond the river you will come to the Hotel Señorial. There will be vacancies there. Tell them I said so. And for the love of God get those children to bed and a decent night's sleep.'

We thank him and creep across the perilously narrow Bailey bridge following the dim, bobbing light of the sergeant's hurricane lamp. And almost exactly seven kilometres beyond the invisible river we find a friendly little country hotel. The cook is preparing to leave for home, but she readily rustles up four tasty steaks, which we enjoy in the cool of the tropical night as we watch geckos hunting on a vine-hung terrace wall. We fall asleep in a cosy, palm-thatched cabana to the sound of quiet voices and a guitar played softly in the garden bar.

During the working week in San Salvador our alarm sounds at 5 a.m. The terrace outside the bedroom window is still in darkness, but the first grey light of dawn is beginning to filter into the garden. The cicadas have fallen silent and a few birds are chirruping softly. By the time we leave for school the sun is full up in a cerulean sky and we have a clear view across the valley to the perfectly matched twin cones of the San Vicente volcano twenty miles away, drenched in sunlight, with pristine white cloud roiling down their sides like white sauce poured on some exotic pudding or suntan lotion over the improbable breasts of a Miss Venezuela.

We swing out of our street into the traffic on the Pan American Highway. Streams of ex-school buses, painted every rainbow colour, decorated with every conceivable style of religious and secular art, sardined to bursting point on the inside with breathless people and festooned on the outside with gesticulating people, lumber in both directions. They are emblazoned with homely names like *Doris* or more exotic monikers such as *Michael Jackson*, and their windscreens are so heavily encrusted with gold and silver transfers that it would be a miracle if their drivers could actually see where they were going. They run on a mixture of diesel and paraffin, and trail dense clouds of choking black smoke. The senility of most of these buses is almost as scandalous as the youth and recklessness of their drivers. There is no such thing as a safety test and one regularly reads newspaper accounts of horrific accidents involving some decrepit juggernaut and an unlicensed sixteen-year-old driver. Whatever the state of such irrelevancies as brakes, steering or the existence or otherwise of tyres with tread on them, they all have air horns of astounding power and I am irresistibly reminded of P. G. Wodehouse's apocalyptic vision of aunt calling to aunt like mastodons across the primeval swamps.

There is a flurry and a trumpeting of mastodons ahead where the motor traffic eddies indignantly around something ponderous and slow-moving, and suddenly we slip back into the colonial past. A huge, heavy wooden farm carreta with its great solid iron-shod wheels, laden with sandías, is labouring up the hill towards Santa Tecla, drawn at two miles an hour by two stolid Brahma oxen. The campesino at the reins nods under a broad, ragged palm-frond sombrero. I have seen these carts in El Salvador, in Guatemala and on the altiplanos of Bolivia and Peru. There are fewer than there used to be, but together with the ox plough they still persist as working realities, not museum pieces.

One of El Salvador's many paradoxes is the contrast between the gentleness of its ordinary people and the homicidal tendencies of many of them when they get behind the steering wheel of a vehicle. Red traffic lights are viewed as no more than suggestions. With two lanes moving rapidly nose to tail along the Paseo Escalón at rush hour, drivers will form a third or even a fourth lane, irrespective of traffic coming the other way. One might expect the oncoming drivers to slow down, but they don't. They simply mount the pavement and proceed at the same speed, scattering pedestrians right and left. Driving home from school on the first day of term I was gobsmacked to see a crowded bus coming at me on the wrong side of the dual carriageway, but by the end of the week it was a sight I had learned to take in my stride. What one doesn't do if one has any sense is become personal or show aggression. A gringo colleague with fluent Spanish pretended to be a policeman to intimidate a driver who had scraped his car. The act seemed to be going well, up to the point where he was felled with a baseball bat by one of the passengers who had crept up behind. The pseudo-cop spent the night in hospital and had to pay for repairs to himself as well as to his car. He was lucky. Many Salvadoran drivers carry pistols in their glove compartments, as a friend of ours discovered to her distress.

Of mixed Texan and Mexican parentage, Linda spoke perfect Spanish and looked very much like the young Elizabeth Taylor. Under the auspices of USAID, she was carrying out a survey of women's job opportunities in El Salvador, and as part of her duties she was sent out with a two-man Green Cross paramedic unit in their pickup truck. As they patrolled their beat on the outskirts of the city they came upon a scene of carnage. A well-heeled motorist in a Mercedes Benz had been forced to stop by a big truck which was slewed across the road loading sand. The motorist blew his horn. The trucker ignored him. The motorist lowered his window and gave the trucker a piece of his mind. The trucker told him graphically where he could shove his Mercedes. The motorist pulled his revolver out of the glovebox and shot the trucker dead. The trucker's wife, sitting with him in the cab, screamed in horror. A gang of workers from the sand quarry rushed out and beat the motorist to death with their shovels.

At this point, enter Linda and her Green Cross boys. Clearly the distraught widow could not have been expected to sit in the back of the truck with the bloody cadavers of her husband and his murderer.

'Señora, you had better ride up front with us. The gringa can go in the back with the deceased. Sorry, Linda, chica, but we know you'll understand.'

Such gruesome stories abound south of the Rio Grande. A colleague at the school tells a tale which has the authentically surreal flavour. A British teacher in an international school in Colombia went on a trip to the jungle and died there. The family in Britain were informed and requested that the body be sent home for burial. The headmaster duly went to Bogotá Airport to receive the corpse from the small regional airline and re-despatch it to the UK with one of the international carriers. Imagine his horror when the cadaver arrived on the luggage belt swathed in brown paper and the remains of cornflake packets.

During a civil war, wealthy Salvadorans were far more likely to vacation in Miami or London than in their own country, but we wanted to see something of El Salvador, though with reasonable precautions. We planned our excursions poring over road maps and carefully stocking the van with food, drink, travel sickness pills and plastic containers of water as extra radiator coolant. In case we were stopped by bandits we placed small quantities of money in our wallets and hid the rest behind a panel in the rear of the van. Several friends on similar trips had been robbed and there was some discussion as to whether the best technique was to stop and submit or drive through at speed and risk being shot. Bearing in mind Linda's experience, we knew that the worst compromise was to stop and argue. Just once on our travels we were detained by guerrillas, courteous young men in battle fatigues, who asked for a modest contribution to their campaign fund. Knowing that the alternative was a bullet through each tyre we gladly contributed a dollar and were even given a receipt.

Our first excursion was to a place that for us, and for many of its own natives, seems to sum up El Salvador, that strange little country which is the smallest, most suffering and most indomitable of all the Central American republics. Cerro Verde is one of El Salvador's last remaining remnants of cloud forest, a jungle on a mountain top some two hours' drive from the Capital. One strikes off the main road at the delightfully named village of El Congo and takes a rough track which climbs through the coffee plantations past little red-roofed fincas half hidden by groves of purple jacaranda, through a rising skein of giddy hairpins to end in a spectacular mirador before which all Central America unrolls like a map, mountain, forest, field and river, to where the southern sea beats on white shell-sand beaches.

The trees here are immemorial giants festooned with Tarzan creepers and colonised by orchids. Toucans brawl and quetzals flit shyly through their feathery tops. The air is crisp and always in motion, and after the steamy heat of the lowlands the blood chills in a moment when drifting clouds obscure the sun. Following one of the several miles of walking trails through the forest we come suddenly upon a rustic platform overhanging a vertiginous drop. Immediately the cloud breaks, and there below in the vast crater of a long-dead volcano is the emerald lake of Coatepeque, less known and even more lovely than Guatemala's famous Atitlán.

The Hotel de la Montaña at Cerro Verde has its own special story which, local friends tell us, is typically Salvadoran in its irony. It began in 1780 when a campesino was working in his field in the valley below. Suddenly, with a terrible shuddering, the earth at his feet split open and began to belch smoke and fire. History does not record what happens to a man's livelihood when his farm becomes a volcano. Within a few weeks, a classic cone had arisen from the valley, almost to the height of neighbouring Cerro Verde. Every day for over a hundred and seventy years the volcano Izalco continued to fling out quantities of pyroclastic material, a pillar of fire by night and a pillar of smoke by day. Its activity was so localised and so constant that it was hailed as a landmark rather than a menace. Ships at sea called it the Lighthouse of the Pacific, made their landfall by it, and came safely to haven at La Libertad on the coast thirty miles away.

In the 1950s it dawned on some entrepreneurial genius that serious money could be made from a tame volcano that was as reliable as a high street bus. He bought the neighbouring mountain of Cerro Verde, mere jungle, for next to nothing, and spent a small fortune building a large and beautiful hotel with a spacious terrace and a glass-walled dining room from which the international jet set could savour the finest gourmet cuisine while being entertained by the antics of a live volcano. The hotel opened with a flourish in 1957, which was also the year when Izalco stopped erupting. Stubbornly dormant ever since, it looms, a burnt-out grey firework, so close that one feels that one could almost reach out and touch it. A few hardy plants have begun to streak its slopes with traces of green. The stones at the crater rim are warm and the merest wisp of smoke trails idly from the summit. 'And all of that,' conclude our Salvadoran friends, 'is so typical of El Salvador.'

The idea of a volcano performing for hotel guests was such an original one that I have often wondered if Cerro Verde might have been the inspiration for Douglas Adams's novel *The Restaurant at the End of the Universe*. In the event, the Hotel de la Montaña has survived, but only just. When we knew it, it was never full except for a business retreat or similar function, and on our very first visit with friends in the October half-term break of 1991 we had it to ourselves. At dinner, eight of us huddled together in a small pool of light in the vast chilly space of the restaurant. The waiter arrived with a gas heater on a small wheeled trolley. We ordered Pilsners for the parents and Cokes for the children and studied the extensive international menu with keen

Izalco, the Lighthouse of the Pacific   *Brizardh/ Bigstock*

anticipation. Those with Spanish assisted those with little or none. The waiter returned and we began to order. At each request he shook his head regretfully and for the first time we heard a phrase that was to become very familiar during our forays off the beaten track in Latin America: 'No hay... there isn't any'.

After three or four such responses we asked 'Qué hay?'

'Chicken.'

'What kind of...'

'Shut up, Will. OK. Chicken for eight.'

'What would you like with it?'

'What's the choice?'

'Rice.'

Already there was the distant rumble of approaching thunder. It was pitch-black beyond the windows and without warning our little pool of light was snuffed out like a candle. We sat huddled in the dim glow of the gas stove. The wind rose to a scream. The thunder bellowed. Blue forked lightning crackled from peak to peak of the surrounding mountains, and the glass box we sat in became an electric cell in a fantastic Frankenstein's laboratory of storm. Then the invisible clouds burst open. There were no preliminary drops and no gradual onset to the deluge. Tons of water cascaded in solid sheets down the windows, flooding the glass-walled garden in the centre of the room. The show was as spectacular as it was unexpected and it must surely have been every bit the equal of the volcanic display for which the hotel had been built.

A Load Of Muck And An Actor

One of the old-time Shakespearean 'heavies', it may have been the great Donald Wolfit, was playing in *Hamlet* at the Wigan Hippodrome.

On a warm Wednesday in summer, when there was no matinee, he wandered off into the pleasant countryside around Haigh and sat down on a sunny bench outside the Balcarres Arms, with a tankard of Marston's and his copy of *The Stage*. The bees buzzed sleepily and it was only when a finger of cold blue shadow finally reached out and touched him that he awoke with a start, fumbled for his gold half-hunter and realised with dismay that it was already late afternoon. The pub, of course, was closed, but in those days villages still had post offices and it was to Aspull village post office that our worried actor found his way.

'Th' bus? Nay, lad, we only have one afternoon bus to Wiggin and that's gone.'

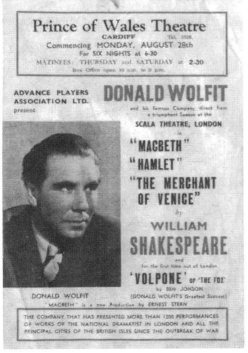

'Oh calamity! This is very distressing. You see, I'm due on stage as Polonius in this evening's performance at the Hippodrome.'

'Ah, *Hamlet*! Well, if I remember rightly, Polonius doesn't come on till Scene Two. I'm sure we can get thee theer befoor that. I'll tell thee what, my brother Jed's a bargee on th' cut. Tha knows, th' Leeds and Liverpool Canal. It runs reight past th' bottom o' Pendlebury Lane and I happen to know as our Jed will be passing any time in th' next half hour. Get thisel down theer and tell Jed I sent thee.'

Ian Redding/Bigstock

'Oh, thank you, thank you, dear boy! I shall be forever in your debt.'

The old thespian did as the postmaster suggested, and within twenty minutes he was comfortably seated aboard the narrowboat *Ludovic Lindsay*, clutching his silver-topped cane, cloak gathered about him and fedora pulled well down against the deepening chill of an English summer evening. It was a short run into town, though with a steep flight of locks to negotiate, and Jed was confident of getting him to the theatre on time. But as he relaxed next to the skipper on the stern thwart of the barge our actor gradually became conscious of a pungent odour rising from the open forward hold. And sure enough, when the keeper at Top Lock called out cheerfully, 'What arta carryin' today, Jed, lad?' the kindly bargee stolidly replied, 'A load of muck... and an actor.'

And as they approached the second lock, the same scene was replayed with exactly the same dialogue:

'What arta carryin' today, Jed, lad?'

'A load of muck... and an actor.'

But as they approached the third lock, the old actor turned to his companion and said gently, 'Jed, dear boy, before we reach the next lock, could we possibly have a word... about the billing?'

CHAPTER 4

BLOODY WOGDIN

Simmons, Ross and I were all of the Junior Committee of the Wigan Rowing Club. In fact, we were slightly more than half of the active members of the club, which, by the early 1960s, had been in decline for many years. The boathouse stood on its own basin just off the Leeds and Liverpool Canal at Haigh quite close to my great-grandfather's old home, Astley's Farm, and overlooked by the bridge carrying the tractor-trailer road through the plantations up to Haigh Hall.

Founded in 1872, the club's regattas had made use of the broad, relatively straight stretch of the canal between the boathouse and the main road bridge at New Springs. They must have been quite a sight in their heyday, with ladies in muslin dresses, gentlemen in straw boaters and colourful blazers and many a keen competition against rival clubs for singles, double sculls and coxed fours. The Leeds and Liverpool is a 'broad' canal, but of course eights would have been impossible to turn and even the fours were challenging enough in this respect.

A major problem of the Rowing Club during its early-1960s decline was that it had hardly any boats, or to be more strictly accurate, it had hardly any boats that were particularly good at doing what boats are supposed to do best, by which I mean floating. According to Simmons, who had been attempting to prop up the club for the past couple of years, a visiting former German Olympic rowing coach had recently wandered into the boathouse, experimentally tapped each hull in turn, muttered 'Es ist kaput' and wandered out again. To put the matter into second-hand-car-dealer-speak, almost all our boats were in need of attention, which was a pity because in their palmy days many of them had been very fine indeed. There was a clinker-built gig whose stern seat had an intricate, high wrought-iron backrest that cried out to be adorned with an Edwardian beauty, languidly twirling her frilled parasol, but our own favourite vessel was a portly, ancient whaler named *Ebb Tide* which Captain Ahab might instantly have claimed for his own. Seventy-year-old Mr Albert Bannister, the only surviving senior member, told us that in the club's great days she had regularly been used by members on their visits to the Crawford Arms at Red Rock.

'Two miles there and five miles back,' said Albert with a solemn wink.

Albert was in the process of restoring the solidest of the Club's 'fours'. Her massively planked sides and fixed thwarts, predating the introduction of the sliding seat in the mid-1870s, made her at least ninety years old. Albert had removed the iron outriggers prior to working on the hull but, in his absence, four of us equipped with canoe paddles surreptitiously launched her and propelled her to New Springs and back, dugout style, raucously chanting Paul Robeson's war song from *Sanders of the River*.

This early period of messing about in boats coincided with the amalgamation of my alma mater, Wigan Grammar School, with the Thomas Linacre School in 1962. School amalgamations, as I know from the one I went through as a deputy headmaster in Lincolnshire twenty years later, are fraught with all kinds of complications, and amongst many other problems the newly combined WGS was temporarily short of PE staff. So when I cheekily suggested to George Merriman, the highly approachable new headmaster, that rowing could be offered as a Wednesday afternoon option, he was immediately interested. And

Wigan Rowing Club

he positively jumped at the idea when I earnestly assured him that as an established club member and an experienced oarsman I would be perfectly capable of supervising the activity without the help of a teacher. (If you are going to tell a lie, make it a whopper and tell it with confidence). Much to my surprise and delight my assurances were accepted without question and for the whole of my lower sixth year a group of us independent spirits joyfully escaped the attentions of Mr Kipling's flannelled fools at the wickets and muddied oafs at the goals, to spend our Wednesday afternoons messing about in boats.

In sober truth, had we ever been tempted to tell it, there were nowhere near enough canal-worthy boats to go round, but we successfully promulgated the fiction that those who were not actually rowing at any given time would be busy repairing craft under my skilled direction. From time to time one master or another was despatched to check up on us, but as we always posted a concealed lookout with a long view of Basin Lane our 'surprise' visitor would arrive to the sound of busily tapping hammers and find a diligent group of craftsmen clustered around an overturned boat supported by three trestles in the centre of the main shed. If he had looked more closely, he might have noticed that it was always the same boat.

The leading light amongst us junior members was John Simmons, the eldest son of the Irish GP who lived at Holly Bank in New Springs. John was even more of a hopeless romantic than I was, and acknowledging that his own head was usually in the clouds he credited me with a wisdom I didn't possess and habitually addressed me as 'Prof'. Our coterie also included Donald Ross, a fellow sixth-former at WGS, who swore more creatively than anybody else of my acquaintance, sang tenor in St George's Church choir, and already had an enviable top B. On the fringes of the group there was an earnest and rather gormless youth called Walkden, inevitably pronounced in the Wigan manner, who also lived in New Springs and whose first name I can't recall because he was invariably referred to simply as 'Bloody Wogdin'. I remember Donald asking John Simmons:

'So what's this Wogdin's first name?'

'Bloody,' came the terse reply.

Strangely enough, it was Bloody Wogdin who provided me with

the only rescue opportunity of my waterborne career. As a professional swimming teacher, my mother Beatrice had ensured that I was competent in the water (though she incessantly disparaged my inelegant 'screw kick') and I had duly acquired the Royal Life Saving Society's Bronze Medallion, a fact which must have contributed to my over-protective parents' non-interference in my boating activities and might have helped to persuade the headmaster that I was a competent supervisor. An old family friend had been honoured by the Society for rescuing the perishing from the murky waters of Liverpool's Albert Dock during the First World War, and at fifteen I was intrepidly poised to do the same if the opportunity ever presented itself.

On the sunny summer afternoon when the big moment came, Simmons and I were setting out for New Springs in *Ebb Tide*. We must have been feeling benevolent because when Bloody asked for a lift we said cheerfully, 'Sure, hop in.' All went smoothly until it was time for him to hop out again. As we were nosing the bows into an eroded part of the bank just short of the road bridge, our passenger leapt suddenly into a precariously upright position on the tiny forward deck.

'Wait! Let Prof get ashore first!' called John urgently but it was too late. As Bloody stepped on to the bank with his right foot the boat slid smoothly sternwards with his left foot still on the foredeck. For an agonizing moment he stood poised in the splits with one foot on the bank and the other on the boat. Then *Ebb Tide* continued her reverse glide and he hit the water with a tremendous splash, yelling 'I can't swim!'

The next few moments were quite literally a flurry of activity. John used his oar to bring the boat into the bank and I, well trained in the dangers of diving into unknown waters, jumped over the side. To my astonishment and, dare I say it, disappointment, the water came up no further than my waist, although our passenger, having sat down, was in every sense of the expression in it up to his neck. Grabbing him unceremoniously by the hair I hauled him ashore and left him muddy and dripping on the towpath. 'Bloody Wogdin,' muttered John dourly as we rowed on damply towards Top Lock.

This was not to be my only ducking in the Leeds and Liverpool Canal. The flimsy single scull shell boat, the rapier of rowing, requires a delicacy of balance which is not acquired by bludgeoning about in tubby old craft such as *Ebb Tide*. With a shallow hull less than eighteen inches wide, the rower's centre of gravity is precariously high. The oar blades are large and curved and the idea is not to lose impetus or balance by 'catching' too deep but to keep a long, steady stroke and then 'feather' smoothly back, skimming the reverse of the blade across the surface of the water. The oar shafts pivot on long outrigger rowlocks, and each stroke produces enormous pressure which is transmitted into forward motion through the hull. Modern boats are made from ultra-light synthetic materials, though of course ours were wooden, though light enough for their period.

Having become reasonably proficient in the double scull with John Simmons, I was eager to have a go at rowing a single scull boat, though I wanted to do it without any critical witnesses to my maiden attempt. So I made a point of cycling up to the boathouse at about nine o'clock on a chilly English summer morning before, I hoped, any of the other members were about. Of the several in the boathouse, only one shell boat seemed to be sound and complete so I lifted her carefully off the rack, launched her into the boathouse basin and shoved off, pausing to screw the oars firmly into the rowlocks. As I sat there in the middle of the basin with the blades resting lightly on the water, something rather magical happened. A large water vole broke the surface, clambered on to one of my oars and proceeded to groom himself, stroking back his whiskers with both delicate paws like an Edwardian masher brilliantining himself for the rowing club ball. It was my first close encounter with Ratty of *The Wind in the Willows*, though one of his Iberian cousins now lives in a pool of the river a kilometre below our house in Andalucía. The canal Ratty didn't appear to notice me at all, and I sat entranced until he had finished his grooming and slid back beneath the surface as noiselessly as he had come.

There was quite a brisk breeze blowing, which threatened to broadside the boat as I edged and handed her into the main waterway through the narrow arch of the little humpbacked stone bridge which carried the towpath. I let the wind take me clear of the bank and into the deep middle of the channel quite close to the high cast iron bridge, over which the tractor-trailer loads of weekend visitors passed on their way from the Plantation Gates to Haigh Hall. Looking up, I realised that my hope for privacy had been frustrated because the first tractor of the day was at that moment rolling to a halt so that its few passengers could get a good view of the solitary, intrepid oarsman. But having come this far I knew that the die was already cast. Looking down again, I noticed a line of tiny water beads forming along what was obviously a lengthwise hairline crack in the bottom of the boat. 'Nothing to worry about there,' I said to myself, much as Captain Smith might have muttered on being told that the *Titanic* had struck the iceberg only a glancing blow. And so saying I threw every muscle and sinew into a flying start which would shoot me through the bridge under the admiring eyes of the spectators, especially the pretty girls in their summer dresses.

But we didn't shoot through the bridge or anywhere else. The sudden pressure on the outriggers opened the bottom of the boat like an unzipped banana. One moment I was poised as it were for Olympic stardom. The next I was up to my neck in the cut. True, the people on the bridge were highly entertained, but not in the way I'd hoped. It is almost impossible actually to sink a wooden boat, especially one as light and flimsy as a single scull, so once I'd recovered my breath it was fairly easy for me to swim crabwise back to the boathouse bank with her thin prow under my arm and then walk her semi-submerged through the little bridge and into the basin. As I cycled soggily back to Whelley, I reflected that even Nelson had his bad days and at least, if I stuck to boating on canals, I'd probably never be seasick, unlike the Hero of the Nile, who suffered horrendously every time he set sail.

The story of my ducking of course went the rounds, and my classmate David Aspey commemorated it in a cartoon in which spectators goggled from a canal bridge at a forlorn and solitary hand just breaking the surface of the water, like something mystic and wonderful from Arthurian legend. For months after that the merest mention of 'Jack's hand' would send my friends into fits of stifled laughter.

One of the consequences of *Ebb Tide* being, like all of our craft, not entirely watertight was that there was always a slowly gathering pool in her bilge, and from time to time we would shift the crew aft to weigh down her stern, move aside the duckboards and bale her more or less dry with a battered tinplate mug. This regular exercise gave me the idea for getting even with the fishermen.

Canal-side anglers and boaters do not mix, the former accusing the latter of disturbing the fish and the latter regarding the former as miserable killjoys who have devoted their lives to a pastime which is only marginally less boring than golf. So whenever *Ebb Tide's* bluff bows were pointed in the direction of Red Rock, a picturesque reach of the cut much frequented by these piscatorial Jonahs, we knew we were probably in for abuse and even bombardment with stones, apple cores, jam butty crusts and the occasional dead cat. If we rowed 'small' like our maiden aunts, and kept to the far bank, we might get away with running the gauntlet with no more than black looks but it was always touch and go.

Our latest bilge-bailing session reminded me that tucked away in a cupboard in the boathouse was an old Victorian iron handpump which was still in excellent order. It worked quite simply. You submerged the inlet valve, rapidly rotated a handle hurdy-gurdy-wise and a plentiful jet of water shot out of the nozzle at the other end. I discovered that by attaching a short aluminium pipe of slightly lesser bore I could greatly increase the pressure and hence the range of the jet.

Removing the midships section of duckboards, we used a bucket over-side to fill the bilge with water to two or three inches in depth. Then John, Don, Bloody and Jimmy, with me at the helm, rowed past the nearest line anglers, hugging the opposite bank and wearing sickeningly respectful expressions. Once hidden by the next bend, the crew rapidly turned the boat through 180 degrees while I abandoned the tiller ropes, submerged the inlet valve and rested the nozzle firmly against the gunwale. Then the oarsmen bent to their sweeps.

She was a heavy boat, but youth and brute force were on our side, and *Ebb Tide* fairly swept back around that bend with a bone in her teeth. This time we had no intention of keeping to the far bank and as we passed within six feet of the startled anglers I cranked the handle for all I was worth. A howl of astonishment and dismay from the enemy and we were away along the far bank, leaving them dripping irately and mouthing foul oaths.

Clearly I enjoyed the rowing, but having been brought up on the stories of Captain Marryatt and Arthur Ransome, I was really a sailor at heart, and while John Simmons was usually the leader in matters nautical, it was entirely my idea to convert *Ebb Tide* to sail. The east-west canal reach between the boathouse and New Springs bridge was more or less straight with only a few gentle curves and there was almost always a light steady breeze blowing in the right direction. This was essential to my purpose because *Ebb Tide's* hull, broad and shallow with no keel to speak of, was completely unsuited to tacking or otherwise manoeuvring under sail, and in any case the width of the waterway would hardly have accommodated it. With the wind behind her I was convince that she would fly, though any upwind work was clearly out of the question. The idea therefore was that we would sail triumphantly down to Top Lock, a mile or so beyond New Springs, lower the mast and row back home. Given that we had already decided that we were not going to attempt anything more complicated than steering in a straight line, there was no point in trying to create a fore-and-aft sail and we were agreed that for the purposes of her maiden voyage under sail *Ebb Tide* was going to be a square rigger.

There was no question of carrying out any major surgery on the boat beyond boring holes in the centre thwart and duckboard to provide a 'step' for the mast, a stout twelve-foot bamboo pole. The forestay, backstay and shrouds supporting it were lengths of clothesline firmly wired to the masthead and secured to the hull with cup hooks, and the yard which was to carry the sail was another shorter and lighter bamboo pole. The sail itself was a miracle of thrift. In those days the waste-making economy

James Williamson/ Bigstock

was in its infancy and my mother, a product of 1930s austerity, threw away very little that could be reused. The sail she donated to our project had started life as two separate sheets. As they had become increasingly worn Aunty Edie had sewn them back to back on her old Singer, creating a two-ply hybrid which was much stronger than the originals. Having seen Edie do the same kind of thing on numerous occasions, I firmly stitched a row of brass curtain rings to the top edge of the sail and single eyelets to each of the bottom corners to attach the 'sheets', which may sound like sails but are in fact the ropes which control them.

'What needeth to sermon of it more?' as Chaucer remarked in quite another context. The day of departure dawned bright and clear as such days always did in the summer holidays of long ago. Simmons, Ross and I, having provisioned her for an epic voyage with such exotic rations as mint balls and bacon and egg sandwiches, clambered aboard and weighed anchor (or rather, undid the painter from its mooring post outside the boathouse). I was quietly chuffed to find that the rig really did work exactly as intended and we fairly scudded before the freshening breeze towards the hitherto uncharted waters of the Top Lock reach.

In those days I was a keen sketcher and I could imagine myself on our return drawing a tongue-in-cheek chart with inscriptions in florid script such as 'Heere bee Dragons'. In the event, as we approached the road bridge the face we saw grinning down at us from the low parapet was more of a gargoyle than a dragon. We absolutely knew, of course, that *Ebb Tide* under sail was the most elegant thing afloat and we were counting on the awed appreciation of an admiring New Springs populace, rather than these ribald sallies of Wigan wit.

'Is that a boat or a washing day? Them sheets is clotheslines and yon sail's definitely a sheet but where's yer mother's knickers then, Proffy?'

'Bloody Wogdin,' muttered John grimly. 'Just wait till I get ashore…'

But no punitive landing was necessary. In calculating the height of *Ebb Tide's* mast I had not allowed for the low clearance under New Springs bridge. As Bloody leaned over excitedly and drew breath for further shafts of wit, the thick bamboo mast stuck him squarely on the nose and squashed it like a ripe plum. We never got to Top Lock but all agreed that it had been a most satisfying voyage.

Christmas Eve In Wigan

From *A Wigan Childhood* by John Sharrock Taylor

In the early years of our marriage, one of our continuing links with the old town was Wigan Parish Church, where I was a member of the choir and drove over for rehearsals and services until our move to Cambridgeshire in 1979 made that impossible. In an era when many all-male church choirs, especially those whose town-centre parishes were suffering wholesale demolition, were shutting up shop, the All Saints choir was still thriving under the directorship of David Cutter. Godfather to our son Richard, David was one of the last generation of Keble graduates to speak with the Oxford accent of Huxley and Professor Joad. Thirty-odd years in Wigan did not manage to erode it but it was even more remarkable that he managed to persuade choristers from Delph Street and Gidlow Lane to sing in the cut-glass tones of Christ Church Cathedral. I recall one Grammar School lad who stubbornly insisted on 'gold, frankincense and MARE' until David pulled him up short.

'Listen, Karl, what do you Wiganers call your civic leader? The fellow with the gold chain?'

Karl paused for thought and then broke into a broad grin. 'Th' MURR,' he replied triumphantly.

'That's it! Keep thinking "gold frankincense and th' MURR" and it'll come out just right.'

In addition to the couple of dozen trebles drawn from several local primary schools, the choir of the 1970s had a strong corps of men ranging from youngsters like myself to veterans such as Eric Harris, Jack Hollis, Arthur Prescott, Harry Talbot and the splendidly named William Henry Sumner Taylor Walker, Wigan's answer to Beniamino Gigli. Like his great hero, and to paraphrase the general confession in the *Book of Common Prayer*, Sumner had a habit of haspirating where he thought not to have haspirated and not haspirating where he thought to have haspirated, and his memorable performance of the tenor solo in

Harold Edwin Darke's beautiful carol 'In the Bleak Midwinter' inspired our colleague John Benn to pen the following gem:

In the bleak mid-winter Sumner made great moan.
Thought he was a tenor (A view which was his own).
Hoh, how we habhor him
Hon this Christmas Day
With his 'hox' and his 'hass'
And his haitches hall hastray.

One of my visits to the Parish Church during the late 1970s stays in the memory not only because it ended in a scene worthy of *Monty Python*, but also because it seemed to sum up my own conviction that the more things changed in Wigan the more they remained essentially the same.

The Christmas midnight mass had just finished and the richly coloured interior of Th' Owd Church was bathed in mellow candlelight. The Rector said the final vestry prayers and the men's choir prepared to process back to un-robe in the song room behind the church. Billy Cowan, the verger, swung open the heavy Gothic door and the lamplight

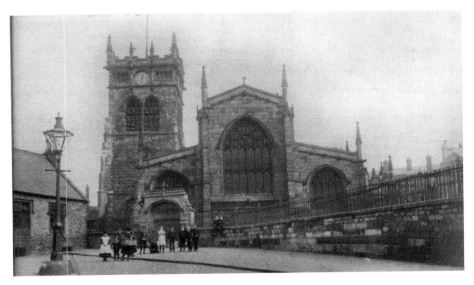

Wigan Parish Church

spilled out into the churchyard. It had been snowing for perhaps half an hour and huge feathery flakes floated gently down on to the worn paving stones and on to a young couple who were feverishly making love right in front of the open door. There was a brief reflective pause, then two of my elderly colleagues delicately lifted the hems of their cassocks and stepped, daintily as duchesses over the prostrate bodies. The couple were so absorbed that several seconds and half the choir had passed before they noticed what was going on. Then they leapt to their feet in embarrassed confusion and fled down the churchyard, the girl covering her face in horror and the young man hopping unsteadily on one leg as he attempted to insert the other into his jeans. He turned and glared fiercely at us.

'What do you lot think you're gawping at?'

Well, I don't think we had any doubt about the answer to that and I can remember supposing that my older colleagues, all round about the age I am now, would be scandalised or embarrassed by the experience. We arrived in the song room and there was another thoughtful pause, then:

'Poor kids! To be as desperate as that!'

'And snowing too!'

'We used to tek our lasses down th' canal bank to do yon. Dosta remember, Jack?'

'We did that, Arthur, but, my God! Never in December.'

'Well, Merry Christmas, all.'

'Aye, Merry Christmas.'

CHAPTER 5

THE LANCASHIRE CARUSO

'Ancora! Ancora!' The young English tenor was delighted. An Italian audience actually begging him to repeat his rendition of the Duke of Mantua's second aria! He threw his whole being into the florid cadenza and hung on to the final top B until he felt his heart and lungs would burst.

'Ancora! Ancora!'

'La donna è mobile' three times and with two hours of *Rigoletto* still to run? 'Grazie, ma scusatemi signori! Non è possibile!'

A voice from the gallery: 'You will sing it and sing it until you get it right.'

Italian opera audiences are notorious for their critical attitude to foreign singers. Some Anglophone imports have gone to great lengths to avoid the pain, though others have simply toughed it out. The great Irish tenor John McCormack, whose mother's maiden name was Foley, made his debut as 'Giovanni Foli' and got away with it because his Italian pronunciation was perfect. The stage directions in *The Barber of Seville* require Count Almaviva to thrash Figaro with a horse whip and the irascible Heddle Nash, 'Nettle Rash' in ITMA parlance, famously did a thorough job on an Italian baritone who had mocked his imperfect pronunciation.

In the early 1960s my grandmother would often exclaim about how the world had expanded since her younger days. While she was clear that not all the changes were for the better, she was equally certain that some of them definitely were. Her transistor radio was a case in point. Her big old valve wireless set, in its walnut cabinet, had taken an age to warm up and, when it did finally achieve operating temperature, often produced little more than the smell of hot dust and a few ghostly mutterings apparently from long-dead foreign stations. In contrast, grandma's new toy only required the touch of one of its big, square, cheerful plastic buttons to bring the pre-set BBC Light Programme flooding jauntily into the glass lean-to which served as a kitchen at 169 Whelley.

Fifty years on from the excitement of those first bulky trannies (an entirely innocent word in those days) I experience a similar small thrill when I turn on my laptop in the morning, because in spite of all the garbage which daily invades my inbox I know I can immediately be in touch with a whole world of knowledge, sounds and ideas. And the moment I wrote those words I realised I was plagiarising somebody. Keats' 'On first looking into Chapman's Homer'? No, in five seconds the Internet comes up with answer that Sir Isaac Newton made a similar point more than five centuries ago, the difference being that, but for the power of his genius, the great ocean of truth would indeed have continued to lie undiscovered before him, whereas I can look it all up on *Wikipedia*.

One of my most useful Internet resources is *YouTube*. Having hammered into the reluctant brains of my choral group the notes and rhythms of 'What Sweeter Music?' I can, Ariel-like, summon out of the ether the definitive performance by the composer and his Cambridge Singers, and declare in no uncertain terms and without fear of contradiction 'This is exactly how Rutter wants it.' *YouTube* also allows me to indulge my passion for opera to what my wife regards as an unnecessarily extreme degree. Forgetting the earphones which would enable her to retain at least a shred of sanity, I can fill the house with ten consecutive, and different, performances of *Tosca*'s 'Vissi d'Arte', before deciding that nobody, not even Magda Olivero and certainly not the wobbly, squalling Callas, does it better than Montserrat Caballé, though young Renée Fleming is not at all bad.

One of the most intriguing *YouTube* phenomena is how clearly it shows that the performances of some of yesteryear's greats 'travel' across time, and some quite emphatically don't. Webster Booth, whose career in light music was swamped by the Rock craze of the 1950s, now sounds vocally as modern as Ian Bostridge. Just listen to his 'Celeste Aida' with the magnificently controlled mezza voce final B flat that Verdi calls for but almost never gets. And if that's not enough, try his duet 'O Soave Fanciulla' with the equally ravishing Joan Cross, both voices rising effortlessly to a pianissimo high C. In contrast the vocally wonderful Heddle Nash, through his dated diction, is firmly anchored in the 1930s.

It is fashionable among greybeards of my generation to lament that the art of bel canto is long gone, but if you share that prejudice simply search out the name Rosa Elvira Sierra and you are in for a rare treat, for this petite young Mexican soprano is the equal of any Tetrazzini or Gall-Curci, whether she's floating impossibly pianissimo top Ds in Gilda's 'Caro Nome' or nonchalantly doubling the flute part in Susanna's 'Deh Vieni'.

When, as a teenager, I first became interested in 'proper' music, my resources for hearing it were very limited. My first 'EP', bought second-hand from an outside stall on Wigan market, was an abridged version of the Tchaikovsky *Piano Concerto in B Flat Minor*, and my earliest vocal was Harry Secombe's recording of 'Nessun Dorma'. Now, if you are a proper opera buff, you may smile indulgently at that, but if you do, let me refer you to *YouTube*, because in addition to an enormous selection from the realms of gold (we're back to Keats again) it gives listeners the opportunity to comment on the performances. Though there are as many versions of Prince Calaf's great aria as there are of 'Vissi d'Arte', ranging from Pavarotti of World Cup fame through Richard Tucker (splendid) to Paul Potts ('pot' as we used to say in my Wiggin youth), the ringing tones of Secombe the Goon are placed high in the ranking order both by folk who remember him and by operatically knowledgeable souls who wouldn't have been able to tell him apart from Mr Pickwick. 'And the point?' I hear you ask. Well, it is simply this: When I were a lad, flat-capped oldsters would intone 'Harry Secombe? You should have heard Tom Burke, the Lancashire Caruso.' Well now I have heard him. Many of his performances are on *YouTube* along with a plethora of recordings by the great Caruso himself. Do they sound alike? Not in the slightest. 'Surely a matter of opinion?' I hear you say. Well, possibly, but only if you are tone deaf and the difference between a narcissus and a nightingale is also a matter for debate.

After Caruso died in 1921, at the height of his fame, the theme of who would be his successor was endlessly discussed, with aficionados of the various protagonists hotly supporting their candidates, though a down-to-earth young peasant from the Marché neatly sidestepped the whole debate with the words 'I'll be the first Gigli, not the second anybody.' Many years later, Mrs Dorothy Caruso gave her opinion that it was Bjöerling who sounded most like her late husband, but what did she know, and what did Jussi care? According to Tom Burke, when Enrico Caruso first heard the young Leigh lad sing he told him, 'One day you will wear my mantle.' But Caruso was a generous man and rather given to expansive statements. Operatic legend records a chance meeting with John McCormack in a corridor of the Metropolitan Opera, New York:

McCormack: Good morning, Enrico, and how is the world's greatest tenor today?

Caruso: Since when, Giovanni, did you become a baritone?

One of nine children, Thomas Aspinall Burke was born at 7 Mather Lane, Leigh, on 2 March 1890. His father, James Vincent Burke, was from Bray, County Wicklow in Ireland. His mother, Mary Josephine Aspinall, also carried Irish genes and it is undoubtedly from this Celtic heritage that Tom's tenor voice derived its brilliant silvery colour which was completely different from Caruso's dark, baritonal timbre.

James Burke worked as a coal miner at a time when industrial disputes caused great hardship to strikers' families, who had to rely on charity soup kitchens and scavenging on the pit dirt rooks for fragments of coal. The anger and frustration of those days, when bread and margarine were the staple diet and poor cuts of meat only a Sunday luxury, stayed with his son all his life, as did an unreasoning resentment of anyone he perceived to be high and mighty. So when, after a triumphant performance, an equerry of King George V came round to his dressing room to say that the king wanted to congratulate him, he replied 'Tell the old bugger he can wait.' He was equally abrasive with illustrious fellow artistes, growling at Martinelli 'Giovanni, you're sounding like a nanny goat, but then, you always did sound like a fucking nanny goat.'

James Burke had a good tenor voice and the Irish songs he sang were the beginning of his son's education in music. Tom was a clever scholar but left St Joseph's Primary School at the age of twelve to make his contribution to the family exchequer, first in a silk mill, then as a 'lasher-on' of coal trucks at a pithead and later, until his early twenties, as a hewer at the coal-face itself. Fascinated by all kinds of music, he joined Leigh Borough Brass Band and in 1904, at only 14, he was promoted to first cornet and won a silver medal for his solo playing in a national

Tom Burke, the Lancashire Caruso

championship at Crystal Palace. A fine sprinter, he played football for a schoolboy team nicknamed, for obvious reasons, the 'Ragged-Trousered Rangers', played rugby as a second row forward and toured Lancashire as an amateur boxer.

Like Harry Secombe in a South Wales mining valley a generation later, Tom Burke received his earliest vocal training in the church choir.

61

He dreamed of becoming a singer, but he and his father were well aware that professional help was necessary to develop his callow voice. Dr Mort, an Atherton teacher, helped him lay the foundations of his technique but it was the Swarbrick family, professional entertainers in a local way, who convinced him that if he really wanted to get ahead he needed to study at the prestigious Manchester College of Music. This would require money both for the tuition fees and the rail fares.

Meanwhile, James Burke decided that the aspiring tenor needed a piano. There was no question of buying one outright, so Mary Josephine's sewing machine went into pawn for the deposit, only to emerge after the instrument had been paid for on the never-never. Even the instalments were only possible because both James and Tom were now making additional contributions to the family economy. James kept pigs and Tom, sent round the pubs with baskets of tripe, had also established his own sideline by singing to the patrons for tips. At weekends he worked as an insurance salesman, as a singing waiter at Leigh's Pied Bull hotel and even (as a boxer he was well able to look after himself) as a debt collector. Thus, in one way or another, the fees and the fares were paid.

Tom Burke's first professional appearance earned him thirty bob (a week's labouring wage in those days) in a presentation of Handel's *Messiah*, a standard work for every northern choral society of the era. His performance was well reviewed in the local press and led to an audition with the Opera Company of J. W. Turner, who told him he was not bad, but not good enough, and needed more practice. Another failed application, this time for the Halle choir in Manchester, led indirectly to a contract with the London impresario Hugo Gorelitz who found him lucrative work in the ballad concerts which, in the days before recording, were used by publishers to promote the sale of their sheet music. Continuing with his studies part-time at the Royal College of Music, Burke became the pupil of a noted singing professor, Signor Levi, who in May 1914 arranged an audition with Caruso, whom Tom had first heard in Blackpool on 29 August 1909. And it was then, or so he said, that his idol prophesied his future greatness, adding, 'You must go to Italy and there you will find your voice.'

Quickly mastering Italian pronunciation, Burke made his operatic debut as the Duke of Mantua in Verdi's *Rigoletto* on 15 December

1917 at the Teatro Lirico in Milan. The break of a lifetime was not long in coming. Having heard him in the same role, the Australian diva Dame Nellie Melba insisted on his partnering her at Covent Garden for the 1919 season under the charismatic baton of another Lancashire Tommy, the great Sir Thomas Beecham. He sang Rodolfo, The Count in *The Barber of Seville* and Pinkerton (not a great tenor role but remember who was the Butterfly). The critics were guarded in their approval, but the audiences were unstinting in their acclaim and Burke's first fourteen pressings for Columbia sold like hot Eccles cakes. It was at Covent Garden that Puccini heard him in the composer's own *Manon Lescaut* on 29 May 1920 and immediately selected him to sing in *Il Tabarro* and *Gianni Schicchi* the following month, exclaiming to the young Mrs Marie Burke: 'I have never heard my music more beautifully sung!' The words, never forgotten, were inscribed on Tom Burke's gravestone almost fifty years later.

For a Lancashire pit lad of 29 who had been at the coal face less than a decade before, what could possibly follow Covent Garden and Nellie Melba? It may be a supreme tribute to Tom's self-confidence that when the Great Lady invited him to join her touring opera company, he turned her down flat, because America was already beckoning. After a shaky start in his native Italy, Burke's hero Enrico Caruso had long since conquered the United States and in the process become the world's first recording superstar. The great Count John McCormack (the title was a Papal honour) had gone a step further, abandoning a stellar career on the operatic stage for the concert platform. The big man from Athlone was a supreme exponent of Schubert, Schumann, Wolf and Richard Strauss, but audiences particularly loved the 'lollipops', the Irish folk songs and sentimental ballads with which he would end his programmes, rendering 'Molly Malone' with same supreme artistry he brought to Schubert's 'Serenade'.

With McCormack, now a US citizen, at the height of his powers, the impresario who organised Tom Burke's first American tour dropped a most resonant clanger when he billed the lad from Leigh as 'The World's Greatest Irish Tenor'. From the very start of the tour, Burke found himself facing audiences packed with rowdy McCormack fans determined to show this young upstart his real place in the tenor hierarchy. The resulting furore wrecked several concerts and did little for the state of Tom's nerves. Fortunately Marie, who was with him on the tour, was able to find enough stage work to tide the couple over a very troublesome twelve months.

The irrepressible Burke soon bounced back, starring the following year at the Chicago Opera and in a remarkably short time he was again touring the American continent and commanding higher fees even than Count John. Returning to Europe in 1927, he went on to appear in Paris, Berlin and Vienna.

Even ugly tenors, and Caruso and Gigli were no oil paintings, have beautiful women fainting at their feet, and Tom Burke in his prime looked very like the young Clarke Gable. His fame, his fortune and his looks all conspired towards his undoing. The pit lad from Leigh fell in love with the champagne lifestyle. Unlike Gigli, who would cheerfully repeat his programme free of charge to entertain the impecunious honeymoon couples in the piazza outside a prestigious venue, Tom became casual about his audiences and frequently failed to turn up for concerts. Ruined by the Wall Street crash, he found consolation in the bottle and by the mid-1930s he was divorced, bankrupt and singing in third-rate musical comedy on Morecambe Pier. Tom Burke died on 13 September 1969, almost forgotten by the operatic world.

Some enthusiasts assert that Tom Burke squandered a talent that might have ranked with his idol, the great Caruso. Those of us too young to have heard him in his palmy days can only judge him by his frankly patchy recorded output, so let's take a last look at *YouTube*. Having invoked Secombe the Goon's 'Nessun Dorma' at the beginning of this chapter, I searched out Burke's version of the same aria, recorded in 1926, the year of the opera's premiere, when he was at the height of his powers. Secombe's performance demonstrates an exemplary smoothness of phrasing and the transition from the long, ringing top B on 'vincero' to the sustained final A, effortlessly riding the orchestral crescendo, is a triumph of both focus and breath control. In his memoirs Beniamino Gigli identifies the one musical skill that cannot be taught as 'the instinctive timing of a musical phrase'. In Tom Burke's 'Nessun Dorma' there is no such timing because there are no phrases. Burke's Italian is a lot better than Secombe's, but his big, bright, dramatic voice with its tight, fast vibrato hammers each note percussively like the prizefighter he once was.

His career virtually over at 42, Burke had repeatedly bemoaned an operatic establishment that slighted singers with non-Italian names. 'If I'd called myself Tomaso Burquio things would have been different,' he told his little coterie of drinking companions at the Pied Bull. It was a hollow excuse for an imagined martyrdom. There were British singers who 'made it' both on the Continent and in the Americas, and one of them, a feisty little lass born in Oldham to parents from Standish near Wigan, became one of the greatest stars in the international firmament.

Saving Corporal Cockrell

Sydney, Jack, Jim and Albert all served in the Great War, and they all lived to tell the tale, though as far as I know, none of them did tell it. Very few soldiers of that war wanted to dwell on the experience. Charles, George, Francis and Henry had no opportunity to tell their story even if they had wanted to. They volunteered in 1914 and were all dead two years later. Sydney, Jack, Jim and Albert were my grandfather and my great-uncles. Charles, George, Francis and Henry were the sons of our village's vicar. The war these eight young men fought in started over a hundred years ago and this is their story.

There are fashions in history as in most other things, and for many years it has been fashionable to decry Britain's part in the First World War as a pointless error perpetrated by war-mongering politicians and by the 'donkeys' who were only too eager to lead millions of heroes to slaughter, always of course from command posts well to the rear. Well, there were heroes and there were donkeys, but it wasn't nearly as straightforward as that and I was pleased to read Jeremy Paxman's recent debunking of what he calls the *Blackadder* view of events. Kaiser Bill may have looked like a harmless lunatic, but many of his invading troops in France and Belgium behaved in a remarkably similar manner to their sons, the Nazis of twenty years later. The war poets also played their part in fudging the issue, from Rupert Brooke's romantic outpourings to Sassoon's iconoclasm. Wilfred Owen got it right when he spoke of the 'pity of war', and even more right when he wrote in 'Strange Meeting' of the tragically vast waste of talent involved in the deaths of those millions of young men.

Even war veterans who are not killed by bombs or bullets often fail to make old bones. I never met my grandfather Sydney or his elder brother Jim, who both died in their mid-forties, and I know them only from sepia photographs and family reminiscences. Albert was invalided out of the West Yorkshires in 1916 with a tumour thought

A Soldier of the King's Royal Rifles, 1914–18

to be malignant. He had the last laugh, surviving another forty years and no doubt outliving the MO who had made the diagnosis.

Sydney, only sixteen when hostilities began, was not demobbed until the war had been over for almost a year. His military record shows him as sober and diligent so I was surprised to find him on a charge for overstaying his leave in the summer of 1919. Then the penny dropped. His pretty young wife Beatrice Adelaide was expecting her first child. The baby, also Beatrice Adelaide, later to be my mother, was born on 22 June and her own twenty-one-year-old mother died the following day. The relevant page of my grandfather's army pay book is stamped 'Charge Dismissed'. Sydney had been a Royal Field Artillery driver, working with the horses that pulled the limbers. A brass-finisher by trade, he didn't return after the war to the cacophony of Wigan's Peppermill foundry, but took on a milk round. 'Bob' who pulled the float was also a veteran, one of the very few war-horses to come home. He dearly loved a band and the sound of the Salvation Army or the local volunteers parading would make him prick up his ears. A little girl in the 1920s, my mother helped her dad deliver the milk.

My paternal grandfather Fred Taylor had worked in a coal mine and died in the Spanish flu pandemic that killed millions after the Great War, so it was great-uncle Jack who became my substitute granddad. Five-feet-two-and-one-tenth inches tall (he insisted on the tenth), Jack Cockrell was an Essex lad who had married Sydney's sister Margaret in 1929. He had started working life as a butcher's apprentice in Colchester, but by the time I knew him he was Superintendent of the Wigan Public Baths. To his staff he was a human fireball who insisted on involving himself in every aspect of their work, and at the drop of any spanner he would exchange his official uniform of black jacket and pinstriped trousers for a set of dungarees and dive joyfully into the mucky coarse sand of the huge steel filters that maintained the water quality of the two swimming pools. Jenny Green, who worked in the laundry, where she taught me to sing Irish protest songs, prophesied 'One of these days Himself will meet himself coming back.'

In spite of this frenetic existence, Jack always had time for me, taking me on long weekend walks with the dogs or rambles over the Welsh mountains, teaching me to look with respect at nature and sitting me on his knee while we read *Tarka the Otter*. A few years later, when I discovered Bruce Bairnsfather's *Bullets and Billets* and his cartoon protagonist Old Bill, with his laconic 'If you knows of a better 'ole you go to it', I eagerly questioned Jack about his time in the King's Royal Rifles:

'Uncle, I know you were wounded in the Great War. How did it happen?'

'I was a quartermaster sergeant. I dropped a shell on me foot.'

This was typical of a quirky sense of humour that I often found puzzling.

Unlike my grandfather and his brothers, all working-class lads, Charles, George, Francis and Henry were public schoolboys from a privileged background. Their father, the Reverend C. H. James, had private means and the three thousand pounds he had personally contributed to the church extension fund was more than forty times a skilled workman's annual wage. The boys' mother Emily was the daughter of a wealthy solicitor and sister of Sir Edward Donner, the Manchester banker, shipping magnate and philanthropist who had managed Winston Churchill's first election campaign. Francis and George had been members of the officer training corps at their schools. When war broke out Francis, an MA in mathematics from St John's College, Cambridge, was on leave from his post as vice principal of a school in India. He and George immediately joined up and shipped out to Egypt with the 5th (Wigan) Territorial Battalion of the Manchester Regiment to train for the Gallipoli landings.

The Dardanelles campaign is notorious as Winston's biggest blunder, and it haunted him for the rest of his long life. The soldiers of the crumbling Ottoman empire were so confidently expected to wither at the first British assault that the Manchesters' training in Egypt had included how to accept the surrender of troops who might not be able to wave the white 'flag' because they didn't possess shirts. Landing at Gallipoli, the Allies found themselves facing a well-armed, well-officered, determined Johnny Turk who was fighting to defend his own land. The Wigan Battalion went into action on 4 June and Second Lieutenant George James was killed the very same day. Lieutenant Francis James, promoted to Captain on 1 August, died six weeks later.

Conscious of their lack of military training, the remaining two James brothers had turned down the possibility of commissions. Charles, a brilliant linguist, who spoke French, German, Italian and Portuguese, was working for the Donner shipping interest in Brazil when war was declared. He immediately returned home and he and Henry, a Dover solicitor, joined the Middlesex Regiment as rankers, though they were quickly promoted. Corporal Charles James was killed at Loos on 28 September 1915, less than a month after landing in France. His brother Henry, 'a splendid sergeant' according to his commanding officer, was officially reported as missing believed killed on 18 August 1916.

Corporal Jack Harold Cockrell, KRR, was not of course injured by a shell falling on his foot. I'm glad to record that he came home and lived another fifty years to found a family and harass the Baths staff with his ferocious energy. And I often think that my own life would have been very different and a great deal poorer if the Mauser round that went in at one side of his thigh and out at the other during heavy fighting near Rouen had found a major artery.

CHAPTER 6

MERRYBALLS

I was a pupil at Wigan Grammar School from 1957 to 1964 and a teacher there from 1967 to 1969, but even if you weren't I hope you will enjoy the three WGS stories in this book.

I think of merryballs as a kind of festive treat, like mint balls or those coloured glass dittos you hang on the Christmas tree. The original term, colemanballs, defined as opening the mouth before the brain is properly in gear, was inspired by the immortal David, with such gems as 'If that ball had gone in, it would have been a goal'. And while the phenomenon is widespread throughout the sporting world, we should never misunderestimate former US Presidents Ronnie and Dubya as stellar exponents in the political branch of the same field. The corresponding Wigan term comes from an odd little story related by Brian Holt who, having been my English teacher at Wigan Grammar School, became my colleague when I joined the staff in 1967. In passing, when I began to write this chapter I had not realised just how many odd little stories and merry-spherical incidents at WGS had actually been catalysed by Brian's wide-eyed and apparently innocent presence.

Patrolling one day on morning break duty, Holt asked a junior boy why he was still in the classroom rather than outside enjoying the fresh air and sunshine with his mates.

'Cos I have to write an essay for Old Merryballs,' muttered the lad bitterly.

George Merriman, the headmaster of Wigan Grammar School, was not an easy man to categorise. 'Shrewd and wise,' said some. 'Utter buffoon,' said others. His detractors claimed he had been appointed by a hostile socialist education authority as a Trojan Horse aimed at wrecking the Grammar School prior to comprehensive reorganisation. His admirers saw him as the first dawning of educational sanity after a long nightmare in the grip of dinosaurs. When he first appeared in 1963, he was immediately faced with the augean task of completing the amalgamation of WGS with its nearest neighbour and bitterest rival, the Thomas Linacre School. As if this were not enough, George carried the additional burden of succeeding the slightly dotty but much-loved Dr Ashley-Smith after a year's interregnum under his deputy, the revered 'Dicky' Nutt, who seemed to have a comprehensive knowledge of every boy who had passed through the school since his arrival as a young Classics master in 1919.

While my WGS merryballs do include some linguistic faux pas, they will also roll quite widely over the considerable range of eccentricity that characterised the school in its final years. In the process I shall certainly give the impression that we were a madhouse in the grip of the more grotesque kind of lunatic, and there is no doubt that both the Marquis de Sade and the directors of the Grand Guignol would have found us a rich source of inspiration. But there were also teachers who undoubtedly knew their stuff. Not a few were inherited from the Linacre, including Len Smith, a great schoolmaster and a true gentleman. I have written elsewhere in this book about Madame Tison and Pop Skirrow. Derek Eccles, happily still with us, was a brilliant teacher with a quirky sense of humour, as was 'Hoss' Jones, a Tolkien buff whose maths club communicated with each other in Elvish. The main problem, as I see it from the long perspective of fifty-odd years, is that the Old Guard was so entrenched that some truly talented younger staff such as the brilliant Geographer McQuade and the English specialist Eric Wells stayed much too short a time, because the path to promotion was so much a matter of dead men's shoes.

One of the Old Guard who earned his salt was Peter 'Paddy' Gore. His individual appearance and studied drawl were absolute gifts to our visual and vocal cartoonists and Paddy employed all the subterfuges of the veteran pedagogue, including the trick of using his bifocals to see what was going on behind him when he was writing on the blackboard. The antics of any luckless sproglet foolish enough to imitate Paddy's hieratic gestures were duly clocked, and in our very first lesson 'Will the little boy who is imitating a windmill please sit down' made a furiously blushing David Sumner drop back into his seat like a small round stone. In the nature of things, much of what Paddy taught in our junior Latin classes only fell into place when I learned to speak Spanish thirty years later, but his History teaching paid more rapid dividends when I won the O Level prize in my fourth year at WGS. A year later, when I was in the sixth form, Paddy's penchant for gesture provided a moment of high farce when he came face to face with the Mad Clapper.

The Mad Clapper was a trader on Wigan's open air market. He was a clapper because he had the habit of clapping his hands together every few seconds. He was mad because he went into paroxysms of fury whenever anybody imitated him, which of course many did. Clapper-baiting was something of a lunchtime ritual with certain WGS boys, who enjoyed it all the more because it invariably ended with the Clapper losing the last remnants of his rag and chasing them flat-footed down Market Street breathing threats and slaughter. Sometimes the pursuit even got as far as the school gates and, on one memorable occasion, beyond them.

Paddy Gore lived opposite the school on the other side of Parson's Walk and often went home for lunch. It was less than a minute's walk to his classroom and he would begin his leisurely stroll back across the quadrangle just before the bell signalled the start of classes. It was in mid-quad on a sunny Friday afternoon that Paddy's path crossed with that of the Mad Clapper. The Clapper's quarry had of course melted severally into the building, and he and Paddy were alone in the wide open space like opposing gunmen on the main street of Dodge City. They paused. Paddy surveyed the Clapper with mild curiosity and the Clapper eyed Paddy with habitual suspicion. And then it happened. The Clapper had only one characteristic mannerism but Paddy had a whole repertoire of them, and one of them just happened to be the habit of clapping his hands together when he was puzzled. By this time the classroom windows on two storeys and two sides of the quad were lined with gleeful spectators. Paddy clapped interrogatively and the Clapper went off like a rocket, dancing with fury and screaming imprecations at this sink of educational iniquity where even the (decorated) masters were in league with the (richly decorated) pupils to fling (handfuls of an odoriferous biological substance) at defenceless members of the public. Paddy, of course, was completely nonplussed, and fortunately Bill Cyclops the caretaker and his brawny assistant had been alerted by the hubbub within the building and were rapidly on hand to prevent the encounter becoming more than verbal. Paddy was still in post at

WGS when I returned there to teach English in 1967 and he gave me an invaluable piece of advice: 'Keep them busy and they'll have neither time nor energy to play you up. Grind them into the ground.'

One younger head of department who had slotted smoothly into the prevailing eccentricity was Geoff Hall, who replaced the horizontally laid-back Tommy Walker as head of Geography. Enormously tall, with a deep, rumbling voice, Hall quite deliberately played up to the kind of pedantic part the sixth-form mimics loved to imitate.

'Make a note of this: Most Norwegian towns…'

'Sir!'

'Shut up. Most Norwegian towns…'

'But Sir!'

'Button it, you squalid nurk.'

'But sir, we're doing Nigeria.'

'Ah… Most Nigerian towns…'

Hall's disciplinary style would certainly have had him arrested in our current era, when the kids rather than the teachers call the shots. Below-par performances in tests were ceremonially castigated with a size-twelve gym shoe called Rupert. The older boys found it all rather entertaining but the small fry were frequently alarmed. The large but notably un-aggressive Brian Holt was surprised to be waylaid one morning at the school gates by a small and very angry young woman. Perhaps her agitation rendered her less than coherent because he thought she was asking if he were Mr Holt. When he said he was, she grabbed him by the lapels and launched into a furious tirade about her first-form son who, she said, clung on to the furniture at home rather than be dragged to school to face his sadistic bullying.

'And you call yourself a Geography teacher!' the distraught mother ended with a fine rhetorical flourish.

'Actually I don't,' replied Brian, who was finally beginning to cotton on, 'I call myself an English teacher.'

'You mean you're NOT Mr Hall?'

'I'm afraid not. My name's Holt. It looks as if we've managed to cross our wires.'

'I am SO sorry.'

'Don't worry. And I'll gladly pass on your message.'

Arriving in the staffroom, Brian was as good as his word. 'Geoff,' he said, 'there's a little lad in 1B who's absolutely petrified of you. It seems that he clings on to the furniture at home rather than be dragged to school to face your sadistic bullying.'

'Does he really? Good.'

After Dicky Nutt's dignified and benignly strict tutelage, George Merriman's first appearance in assembly was something of a shock: tall, gangling, bald, with pointed Mr Spock ears, a friendly smile and the iciest blue-eyed stare I have ever quailed under. He wore a baggy outfit of some faded nondescript colour which we immediately dubbed the Demob Suit and his voice was a deep bass redolent of his Birmingham origins. The school's distinctive architectural feature was its clock tower and having noted George's leisurely Brummie vowels the wags took great delight in constructing such statements as 'I've been wandering near the terrr, picking the flerrrs, for errrs and errrs and errrs.'

George was by turns extremely canny and perplexingly vague, and one of his more endearing characteristics was his ability to laugh at himself. On one occasion I was sitting in the staffroom marking a pile of books when he came in with a broad grin and announced: 'I needed to call the Education department but I inadvertently dialled the school number. The phone rang in the secretary's office next door so I went in and answered it. Yes indeed, I rang myself up.'

George's ability to put his foot in it was legendary. During my second year as a master at WGS one of the Maths staff, off school with a protracted illness, was replaced by his petite young wife, who in the hothouse atmosphere of an all-male establishment became the focus of the kind of fantasy which was only heightened by her appearance in the sixth-form Christmas revue wearing a scanty bikini and pursued by Paul Lowe, the Head Boy, got up as a caveman complete with papier mâché club. Mrs Halewood's normal outdoor wear was a striped jacket with a pointed hood which made her look remarkably like the children's TV puppet Andy Pandy. The school naturally preferred a more erotic version of the name, and Randy Dandy, who was every bit as effective at teaching sums as she was at exciting adolescent lust, became a great favourite with boys and staff alike, as George's remarks in assembly on the last day of term graciously acknowledged:

'What can I say about Mrs Halewood other than that we've *all* enjoyed *having* her?'

The assembly spluttered into its collective handkerchief and Brian Holt, standing with me at the back of the hall, raised his eyes to Heaven then slowly covered his face with an expressive hand.

Dicky Nutt finally retired in June 1967 and Jack Sharratt, his replacement as deputy head, could not have been more different. Dicky had never needed to raise his voice in a crisis because with his well-oiled administration there had been no crises. Jack went red in the face and screamed like a diva whenever things went wrong. And with Mr Sharratt things invariably *did* go wrong, so 'Jack's briefcase' soon became the school's shorthand for 'Limbo'. Holt, a quietly ruthless staffroom bard, put it like this:

There is a man called Sharratt
With a complexion like a carrot
Who'd like to be efficient if he could.
The degree of his efficiency
Falls short of the sufficiency
Required for boiling eggs or chopping wood.

Headmasters inhabit ivory towers and think great thoughts. Deputy headmasters do the real work, and one of their many challenges is the running of the annual public examinations, which in the period I am writing about were of course the GCE O and A Levels. Jack invariably made a complete merryballs of this and never less so than in the case of the O Level English Language exam of the 1968 November retakes. The question papers were supposed to be kept in a safe in the school office. The humble rank-and-file teacher who invigilated the exam did not of course have access to the key of the safe, so his first job was to settle the candidates down and give out the stationery. Meanwhile, that august personage the deputy headmaster would calmly proceed to the office, unlock the safe, retrieve the question papers and process with them at a stately pace into the hall.

As the first invigilator on the day in question, I did my preliminary stuff and waited for Jack to produce the papers. When, after five minutes,

Wigan Grammar School

they had not arrived, I sent an SOS to the deputy head's office, but it was another quarter of an hour before Jack materialised, his wattles an even more than usually interesting shade of puce. After the exam was over Enid, the school secretary, told me the reason for the latest debacle. Jack had not bothered to follow the examining board's strict instructions to lock the question papers in the safe but had merely shoved them at random into one or other of his three desk drawers. Delving into the mass of buff envelopes five minutes before the English exam was due to start, he had been unable to find the relevant packet. He had spent the next ten minutes tearing out the remains of his hair before it occurred to him that bulky documents often slid down the back of overfilled drawers. So he withdrew all three drawers and tipped them out on to the carpet. He was on his knees desperately sifting through their contents when Enid's anxious voice spoke from behind him: 'Mr Sharratt, there's a gentleman here from the Joint Matriculation Board. He says he wants to inspect our arrangements for the security of the question papers.'

Jack was a Maths teacher by trade, so Brian the Bard commemorated the incident in appropriate terminology:

When Sharratt was in the main hall
You could see he was having a ball,

His organisation
Of examinations
Being half the cube root of fuck-all.

Head teachers invariably regard themselves as 'good pickers' and pride themselves on their ability to choose staff, but most of us realise that occasionally we get it spectacularly wrong. Noddy Leigh's appointment at WGS was a merryball of planetary proportions, though George Merriman was as innocent of the resulting chaos as the rest of us, as it was his predecessor Dr Ashley-Smith who had dropped the astounding clanger of appointing Mr Leigh, who looked uncannily like the Right Dishonourable Michael Gove, a fact which, these days, would give pause to any sane interviewing panel.

I have two pieces of advice for any of my younger readers who may be thinking of going into teaching. The first and most urgent of these is 'Don't'. The second, for those reckless enough to ignore the first, is 'Whatever else you do, try to avoid unconscious mannerisms.' The chaplain of a big psychiatric hospital once told me that in preaching in chapel he had learned to keep his hands hidden in his surplice sleeves to avoid making gestures which could be gleefully imitated by the inmates. The same caveat applies in teaching, as Paddy Gore had discovered when he fell foul of the Mad Clapper – and in schools the inmates are usually much more deadly and unpredictable than those in lunatic asylums. Geoff Leigh, and any headmaster mad enough to consider giving him a job, would have benefited greatly if he had observed either rule, especially the first. Imagine a super-intelligent robot with a fixed Gove-like stare, burbling polysyllables at eleven-year-olds in a metallic tenor and punctuating every arcane remark with a manic spasm of the head, and you will begin to get the picture.

Paddy Gore was no intellectual but he was an effective teacher. Noddy Leigh had a brain like a planet and couldn't teach for mint balls. At this point I'm tempted to gallop off on one of my string of hobby horses, but Val is looking disapprovingly over my shoulder so I'll rein myself in. Children know very quickly whether they or the new teacher will be in charge, and Noddy's third-form German beginners had him classified and skewered like a beetle in the first five minutes. Part of the problem was that grammar school lads were supposed to be bright, and Noddy had assumed that they would behave accordingly.

'I should not be obliged to harangue boys of your putative intelligence with such sanctimonious pontification,' he admonished them sternly.

'Ponctimonious santifiwhat, Sir?' they queried and Noddy, knowing he was being guyed, and mis-applying the Paddy Gore dictum, flung himself into the offensive. In those days, masters were allowed to cane, and Noddy wildly and inexpertly thrashed whole job lots of bottoms while the rest of the class stood by and cheered. Strangely, they never seemed to hold it against him. On the contrary, they were clearly fond of him and on one notable occasion they chaired him round the quadrangle singing 'God Bless our Noddy' to the tune of 'God Save the Queen'. Discipline in those dark days was a strictly private matter, and Brian Holt would not have dreamed of intervening if he had thought a master had been present, but the raucous third form cheering from the German classroom suggested otherwise. Peering in through the 'judas' window in the door all he could see was a pulsating mass of humanity piled up in a corner. Picking off each body in turn, he finally reached the bottom of the scrum and discovered that a teacher, of sorts, had been there all the time.

Noddy's eccentricities and his mighty intelligence clearly made him something of a staffroom outsider, and the naturally gregarious Holt decided to take him under his wing and attempt to facilitate his integration into the mainstream of the human race. Until his marriage, Brian had had something of a reputation as a ladies' man. Many of his former flames clearly remembered him with affection, and when he and Noddy entered a crowded bar one Saturday evening they were hailed by one such ex-inamorata who was sitting at a table with her new fiancé and friends. She rose and kissed Brian warmly on the cheek. Greetings were exchanged all round and a diamond engagement ring duly admired. Noddy watched the proceedings with minute interest and as the young woman turned to rejoin her friends his penetrating metallic tenor rang through the room: 'I presume you've had sexual intercourse with that woman?'

The day dawned when Noddy Leigh finally concluded that joining the human race was a bridge too far, so he went off to hobnob with fellow robots in the new language laboratory at Preston's Harris College. With the hindsight of experience, I conclude that he must have been a borderline Asperger's subject, a role Martin Clunes plays so brilliantly in the *Doc Martin* TV series. Surveying his third form delinquents for the last time, he demanded metallically:

'I suppose you all think master-baiting is tremendous fun.'

'Oh yes, Sir!' they chorused gleefully.

The appearance of Noddy Leigh's successor in assembly on the first day of the new term galvanised the reprobates into full attention, because, from a distance, Mr Wilson was the spitting image of Noddy himself, a fact which made the assembled master-baiters mutter 'Noddy Mark Two!' as they rubbed their sweaty palms together and whetted their rudimentary wits with predatory glee. They were in for a shock, because Ken Wilson turned out to be a natural killer who made Hall, Paddy and Basher Collins look like a trio of choirboys. Ken's fourth-form class staggered ashen-faced into my room at the beginning of period two and spilled the beans:

'Sir, he's awful.'

'Who's awful?'

'This new Noddy, Sir.'

'Watch it!'

'Sorry, Sir, this Mr Wilson.'

'Awful? How, awful?'

'Very awful, Sir.'

'No, fool, I mean awful in what way?'

'Well, Sir, he started off by writing a question in French on the board and then he started counting: cinq, dix quinze, vingt...'

'What's wrong with that? It was a French lesson, wasn't it? What did the counting mean, anyway?'

'They were lines, Sir. Long, hard lines in French to be learned by heart and translated by the whole class. It's a system he has. The number of lines keeps going up in fives until somebody has a shot at answering the original question.'

'And something else Sir...'

'What?'

'He knew exactly what we were thinking even before we did. We thought we were in for some fun but this is going to be the term from hell.'

All agreed with that assessment and one lad added thoughtfully, 'I reckon this Mr Wilson must have been working in a borstal before he came to torment us.'

'On the right lines, but you're not quite there,' I replied.

'You mean you actually know what he was doing before he came here?'

'Yes, I do.'

'What was it, Sir?'

'Army Education Corps.'

'Aldershot?'

'A bit further away than that. And not British Army either.'

'What army?'

'The French Foreign Legion.'

This confirmed what they had already known from the first five minutes of Ken's first lesson. There would be no messing with Noddy Mark Two. Not now. Not ever.

The boys in those days gave nicknames to most of their teachers and 'Bird Man', Ken's sobriquet, is easily explained because he was an avid ornithologist, whose solitary suit was liberally spattered with guano. Val and I, recently married and of course still childless, were amused when the Wilsons even named their firstborn son after a seabird, though we gave a firm veto to their attempt to park week-old Dunlin on us while they went off on a birding trip. Ken had a tender hand with the feathered fraternity, and people were always bringing injured birds to him in the hope that he could nurse them back to health. Barney the Barn Owl was a case in point. Barney arrived with partially paralysed feet, which Ken had gradually and patiently manipulated back into almost perfect working order. He wasn't quite ready to be released back into the wild and rather than leave him at home Ken brought him into school each day. The personal lockers in the staffroom had doors which did not reach up to the top of the door frame but left a six-inch gap, so in lesson time Ken would usually leave Barney sitting on the hanger bar of his locker and staring fixedly over the top of the door. The boys were of course fascinated by Barney and just occasionally Ken would take him into class, parking him on a portable perch which he placed on his desk facing the blackboard. His favourite joke on those who had not previously met the owl was to say to the bird: 'Barney, I've just got to pop out for a minute or two. I've left the lads some work and I want you to let me know if anybody talks or does anything he shouldn't do.' Naturally, the moment after Ken had left the room somebody spoke and the owl immediately swivelled his neck through 180 degrees and fixed the culprit with a fierce round-eyed stare. One of the few occasions on which I ever saw George Merriman disconcerted was when he had carefully pinned a new notice to the staffroom bulletin board. Unbeknownst to him, Barney the Barn Owl had intently watched the operation over the door of his cupboard. As soon as the headmaster had inserted the last drawing pin, Barney launched himself into a soundless glide and, grasping the picture rail above the board with his recuperating talons, defecated deftly down the centre of George's announcement. Clearly, in one respect at least, WGS was fifty years ahead of Hogwarts.

At school George Merriman was famous for his ferocious energy, though his wife Dora happily revealed that when he was at home he did little else but sleep. Many wondered how he would cope when retirement came, but we need not have worried because George never retired. He was of course an extremely active year-round Chairman of the Wigan Music Festival, compering the annual events in inimitable terrrs, flerrrs and errrs style. When I saw him at a final day concert in about 1990 he was limping slightly. I knew he had turned eighty and I wondered if age was at last beginning to catch up with him.

'A touch of rheumatism?' I enquired sympathetically.

'No, I was kicked.'

'Kicked!'

'It was an accident.'

'How on earth did you manage to get kicked?'

'I was refereeing a rugby match.'

In The Beginning Was The Nerd

My last job in international education involved setting up two spectacularly luxurious boarding schools financed by wealthy Indian entrepreneurs. This is an excerpt from my book *No Baboons in India*, which tells that story.

The Nerve Centre was a reverentially hushed temple at the very centre of Erkon World School where a team of intense, hawk-like, bespectacled young men sat at a long, curved control panel bristling with switches and coruscating with coloured lights. Immediately in front of them a line of monitors supplied current information about all aspects of the school's technical systems, while above their heads another row of plasma screens relayed closed circuit TV images of every area of the campus. Any variation in temperature, air quality or the chemical analysis of the mineral water supplied to the corridor dispensers would immediately be detected and rectified. Any student experiencing the slightest glitch with her laptop or his Blackberry phone would only have

Nerve Centre   *Ton Snoei/Bigstock*

to call the Nerve Centre's emergency number and an intense hawk-like young man would speed silently to the rescue. Ms Dinraver, planning a PowerPoint presentation in the school's impressive Lecture Theatre, would merely give a couple of days' notice and a similar young hawk would not only supply the necessary graphics from the Nerve Centre's extensive databanks but also ensure that our elegantly supercilious Art teacher's presentation went off hitch-free without her immaculately manicured hands ever having to touch a single button. This, at least, was the theory. Like Alpha Centauri, the reality was some light years away.

As Director of Erkon World School I might occasionally show how choleric I was and make my bondmen tremble, but this little corps of techy trekkies was an entirely different matter. The well-paid Adams of Erkon World School, they had all been installed in Papaji's technological Eden at least two years before the first teacher had set foot within its hallowed portals, and they considered themselves answerable only to the Deity himself on his personal cloud of being in a far-off Delhi suburb. As far as the least of them was concerned all the students' laptops could crash with impunity and even Ms Dinraver, our seductive young Art teacher, could stamp her elegantly-shod foot until she went into a full Bollywood dance routine before they would even deign to take notice.

I confess that I was at a loss. If I made an early call to the emergency number, a remote and reproving voice would inform me that it was merely there to record calls, as all its colleagues were at breakfast. If I called half an hour later they had been summoned urgently to morning coffee. Or lunch. Finally I mentioned my frustration to Ruth, my personal assistant. She had worked for the Erkon organisation for years and was not the least bit impressed by Papaji himself, whom, with his love of gadgets, she often referred to as 'the boy with his toys'.

There was a sharp intake of breath and Ruth's eyes opened wide in disbelief as she picked up the telephone. 'NERD Centre? This is the Director's personal assistant. Kindly inform the Chief NERD that he is required immediately in the Director's Office. At lunch? Then he has two minutes to bolt his chapatti and present himself here. I am counting.'

In fact that exalted personage the Director of Technical Services, a tall imposing Sikh, arrived in my office in well under sixty seconds, though the full two minutes had elapsed before, under the disapproving gaze of my personal assistant, his heart-rate steadied and his breathing returned to something like normal. It was not that he expected Ms Ruth to shave off his whiskers and unravel his pugree. She didn't need to resort to anything so crude. In India the Mata is a revered figure and in Erkon World School, in spite of her title and her bling, it was not Mamaji who was the mother figure.

'Respected Sir. What is your problem.'

'Sex,' I replied tersely.

'Sex?' The Chief Nerd was visibly alarmed.

'Sex. I was attempting to look up a person called Napoleon Bonaparte on a historical web page. The search box required me to specify the sex of the target subject. I immediately received an on screen message from your bloody Net Nanny programme threatening to report me to my boss for attempting to access a pornographic site.'

'Respected Sir, it will be rectified immediately.'

The Chief Nerd was true to his word. Within five minutes my telephone rang and a cheerful voice greeted me from the Nerve Centre.

'Respected Sir, I have made the required adjustment to the Net Nanny programme. You can now access your pornographic site.'

CHAPTER 7

THE MAN WHO KILLED A KING

My ancestors were ordinary folk, such as farmers, miners and brass finishers, but my grandchildren, Richard's children Joseph and Claire, are descended, through their mother, from the brother of Colonel Daniel Axtell, who was hanged, drawn and quartered for 'Imagining and Encompassing' the death of King Charles I. In 1660, on the eve of his Restoration, the dead king's son issued a manifesto from Breda in the Netherlands where my other son Will and my granddaughter Jaya now live.

King Charles I's most notable achievement was to get his head chopped off. This piece of radical surgery, carried out by a masked and anonymous executioner, occurred on an improvised platform outside Inigo Jones's Banqueting Hall in Whitehall one chilly morning in January. In fact, Charles's exit was doubly notable. First, all who witnessed it, even his bitterest enemies, agreed that it was a theatrical triumph well worthy of an Oscar, if that award had existed in 1649. In an ode acclaiming Oliver Cromwell's triumphant return from massacring the Irish, the puritan poet Andrew Marvell, who might have been expected to be hostile to the king, praised 'the Royal Actor' who:

> ...nothing common did or mean
> Upon that memorable scene,
> But with his keener eye
> The axe's edge did try
> And bowed his comely head
> Down as upon a bed.

Charles had spent weeks rehearsing for his final performance. Remote and majestic at a distance, he had a knack of making friends close to. Fearing yet another escape, his captors had provided him with doctrinaire Roundhead servants who could be relied upon to resist this

unlikely ability, but most of them quickly became devoted to the captive king. The last one of all, Charles's dresser for this positively final appearance, recalled with admiration that on the morning of his execution the king asked for two shirts because, 'The season is so sharp as probably may make me shake, which some observers may imagine proceeds from fear. I would have no such imputation.'

Charles I's exit was unique in a second way. In the past, inconvenient kings had been quietly bumped off, but this English revolution was no hole-in-the-corner affair. No other monarch in English history has ever been publicly tried, sentenced and executed. The legality of it has been hotly debated ever since, but all can agree with Major General Harrison when he faced his own grisly death a dozen years later, that 'the things that have been done have been done upon the Stage, in the sight of the Sun.'

King Charles was his own worst enemy. Self-righteous, arrogant, unscrupulous, duplicitous and delusional, the key to his tortuous character was his absolute belief in the Divine Right of Kings, the ancient doctrine that the monarch was answerable only to God. Nine days before his death, he told his judges: 'The liberty and freedom of the people consists in their having those laws by which their life and their goods may be most their own. It is not for having share in Government. A subject and a sovereign are clean different things.' It was a conviction which had led to the biggest series of political blunders ever perpetrated by a British monarch and to one of the bloodiest series of civil conflicts in our history.

There is a scene in Ken Hughes's splendid 1970 film *Cromwell* where Richard Harris's Oliver tries to persuade Alec Guinness's Charles of the virtues of 'a system of government called democracy'. This, as Henry Ford would certainly have told you, is bunk. Only madmen such as the Levellers and the Diggers – led, incidentally, by a Wigan man called Gerard Winstanley – went in for that sort of communistic claptrap. What the middle and upper class parliamentarians of the 1640s insisted on was their ancient right to be consulted about the way the king intended to spend the tax money he demanded from them. The king might be the Producer of the national pageant, but the parliamentarians were the Angels, the backers who kept a firm grip on the purse-strings. They were also more than willing to serve as critics of the royal performance.

After seventeen years of mutual provocation, the final catastrophe of the tragedy was sparked on 4 January 1642 by an astounding breach of parliamentary privilege, when Charles made an unscripted entrance into the House of Commons to arrest five Puritan members whom he accused of sedition. The wanted men had slipped away by boat shortly before the King arrived with an armed guard, and when Charles demanded to know their whereabouts Speaker Lenthall famously replied 'May it please your Majesty, I have neither eyes to see nor tongue to speak but as this House is pleased to direct me.' The scene is commemorated annually when the Commons symbolically refuse to admit the monarch's messenger, Black Rod, when he summons them to the state opening of Parliament. For Charles himself it would create a more pointed precedent when, seven years later, the 'purge' of the Commons by Colonels Thomas Pride and Daniel Axtell would set the stage for the king's own trial for treason.

Hardly anyone on the Parliamentarian side took up arms in 1642 with the idea of deposing the king, much less of executing him. The dilemma was summed up by the Earl of Manchester: 'If we beat the King ninety-nine times he is king still, and so will his posterity be after him; but if the King beat us once, we shall be all hanged, and our posterity be made slaves.' But Oliver Cromwell, a middle-aged Huntingdon squire who had discovered a surprising aptitude for soldiering, replied: 'If the King chanced to be in the body of the enemy, I would as soon discharge my pistol upon him as upon any private man.' It was in this spirit that Old Noll created that perfect instrument of victory, the New Model

Army. His recruits were neither effete aristocrats nor the decayed serving-men and tapsters he had despised among Manchester's troops, but men of spirit, fired by burning religious zeal, men such as Daniel Axtell, a twenty-year-old grocer from Berkhamsted in Hertfordshire. Like Cromwell himself, Daniel had no military background, but he learned quickly. He fought as an infantryman at the battle of Marston Moor on 2 July 1644, where the Parliamentarian forces crushed Prince Rupert's army and effectively annihilated the Royalist cause in the north of England. Less than two years later he was a major in Hewson's regiment, serving with distinction in the campaign against the Cavaliers in Kent.

Money was not the only issue between Charles and his critics. Throughout his reign the King had striven to force nationwide adherence to the Church of England, but in this, as in most things, he was out of step with the age, for thousands of his most radical subjects were Puritans. Aristocratic and middle-class Puritans, such as the members of both houses of Parliament, tended to be Presbyterians and were in favour of a national church as long as it was *their* kind of national church, but many of the Army's soldiers were born-again Independents who despised organised religion. They believed that every man who could read should study the Bible and expound it to those of his brethren who could not read, which is why we find the Baptist Daniel Axtell preaching in Royalist Oxford in 1646, having unceremoniously bundled the lawful incumbent out of his pulpit. All Puritans despised the 'popish' candles, crosses surplices, smells and bells beloved of the king and his archbishop, William Laud, but the most contentious issue of all was the Anglican Book of Common Prayer itself, and King Charles I was quite literally prepared to die to preserve it.

Putting a final end to hostilities proved to be no simple matter. Defeated and captured, the King tried to play his enemies off against each other. First he threw in his lot with the Scots who soon realised he was impossible to deal with and sold him to Parliament, which also failed to persuade him to agree to a constitutional monarchy. Then the Army kidnapped him from his nonplussed Parliamentary captors and spent a frustrating year attempting to negotiate with him before an exasperated Cromwell finally exclaimed: 'I will cut off this King's head

89

with the Crown upon it!'

It was no idle threat, but Oliver was well aware that there would be no majority in Parliament for this most radical of final solutions. So on Wednesday, 6 December 1648, Colonels Thomas Pride and Daniel Axtell led a company of heavily armed soldiers into the House of Commons and forcibly removed more than 250 members. Next to the Palace of Westminster there were three pubs called Heaven, Hell and Purgatory. Though Purgatory might have seemed more appropriate, some of the arrested members were obliged to spend the night in Hell, before being packed off home with their tails between their legs. The stage was now set for the trial and execution of the king.

The trial of King Charles I was an elaborately choreographed affair conducted in an atmosphere of high tension, and John Bradshaw, the President of the Court, wore a hat reinforced with iron plates as a precaution against assassination from the boisterous and divided public gallery. One who had absolutely no doubt about the guilt of the accused was Lieutenant Colonel Daniel Axtell, and his superiors had allotted to him a key role in the drama. As Captain of the Guard his official responsibility was for public order, but like many an amateur actor he succumbed to the temptation to improve on the script, and his ad-libbing would eventually land him too in the dock.

Two hundred thousand people had perished in eight years of civil war, and his prosecutors were determined that all the blame should light upon the head of Charles Stuart, that Man of Blood. As always, the king's enemies were deeply divided as to what should be done with him, and of the 135 commissioners appointed to judge him only 68 actually turned up. Cromwell's military superior, Sir Thomas Fairfax, Lord General of the Army, was one who refused to have anything to do with the proceedings and when his name was read out Lady Fairfax, who was sitting in the gallery, cried out 'He has more wit than to be here!' And when Bradshaw demanded that the king answer the indictment 'in the name of the Commons of England Assembled in Parliament and the good People of England', the same voice rang out again: 'It is a lie! Where are these *good* people? Oliver Cromwell is a traitor!' There was uproar as Colonel Axtell commanded his soldiers to level their muskets at the gallery. Much was to be made of this incident when Daniel faced his own accusers twelve years later. As Captain of the Guard he could reasonably argue that he was only doing his duty of keeping order in court, but the fact that he also encouraged the same troops to call loudly for 'Justice!' was harder to explain away.

The king's imperturbable calm in the face of his accusers clearly unnerved them.

'Know you not that stand before a court of justice?' Bradshaw asked him in exasperation.

'I see that I stand before a *power*,' replied Charles, drily. Naturally, he refused to recognise the legality of the proceedings, and his ironic interjections underlined his quiet boast that he knew 'as much law as any gentleman in England'. In a bid to shut him up, Bradshaw promised that he would be given the opportunity to speak after the verdict had been given. It was a lie. As soon as the death sentence had been passed, the king was hustled away through the ranks of Colonel Axtell's soldiers. As he passed they burned grains of gunpowder on their palms to make smoke to blow in his face. At a signal from their commander they broke into renewed cries of 'Justice!' but now a new and more damning word was added to the chant: 'Execution! Execution! Execution!'

The death of King Charles did not bring about peace. There were continued risings, one of which led to the bloody battle of Wigan Lane in 1651. Continued Royalist agitation in Ireland led directly to Cromwell's determination to 'pacify' it, and indirectly to the four centuries of sectarian 'troubles' which followed. Once again, Colonel Daniel Axtell was to play a prominent and controversial part in the scenes which ensued and there is an intriguing pattern to be observed throughout the campaign.

Daniel sends his troops to capture Grannagh Castle. They fail, so he rides out himself with a couple of siege guns and gives the defenders the stark alternatives of surrendering or being put to the sword. They capitulate and are spared. Later, Cromwell storms the heavily defended port of Drogheda. The Royalist governor and others retreat to a heavily fortified citadel on Windmill Mount. Colonel Axtell promises them their lives if they surrender, but Cromwell refuses to ratify the pledge and they are massacred along with over three thousand other men, women and children. A year later, Axtell, who has defeated the Royalist

A N
EXACT and moſt IMPARTIAL
ACCOMPT
O F
The Indictment, Arraignment, Trial,
and Judgment (according to Law) of
Twenty Nine
REGICIDES,
T H E
Murtherers
Of His Late.
SACRED MAJESTY
Of Moſt Glorious Memory:
Begun at Hicks-Hall on Tueſday, the
9th. of October, 1660. And Continued
(at the Seſſions-Houſe in the Old-Bayley) until
Friday, the nineteenth of the ſame Moneth.

Together with a SUMMARY of the Dark, and Horrid
Decrees of thoſe Cabaliſts, Preparatory to that Helliſh Fact.

Expoſed to view for the Reader's Satisfaction, and
Information of Poſterity.

London, Printed for R. Scot, T. Baſſet, R. Chiſwell
and J. Wright, 1679.

defenders in a daring night attack on Meelick Island in the Shannon, is court-martialled by Cromwell's son-in-law, General Henry Ireton, for allegedly allowing prisoners to be killed after a promise of quarter. Like Cromwell, Ireton had emerged as one of the 'grandees' of the Army who had become increasingly estranged from the Independent rank-and-file. Daniel Axtell was never a grandee either in status or temperament. He had already clashed with Ireton over the general's attempts to suppress the freethinking Baptists, and the Meelick incident was such a reversal of Cromwell's behaviour at Drogheda that some historians have suggested that Daniel was being set up as a scapegoat for the actions of his superiors. Either way, he must have thought 'Damned if you don't, damned if you do.'

Daniel's life continued to be dramatic. Sent back to England in disgrace, his ship was captured by a Royalist privateer and he was imprisoned in the Star Fort on St Mary's in the Isles of Scilly. Irish troops in the garrison were all for stringing him up but were persuaded to spare his life because of their own precarious situation, and indeed Daniel was rescued when the great Puritan Admiral Blake captured Scilly a month later.

England was a republic for only twelve years. When Oliver Cromwell died in 1658 the Protectorate government fell apart, and after two years of political tail-chasing the son of the executed king was invited by a self-appointed committee to return as King Charles II. Not everyone was in favour, and Daniel Axtell was among the veterans who responded to General Lambert's last desperate attempt to rally opposition to the Restoration. Daniel escaped from the fight at Daventry during which Lambert was captured but was himself arrested shortly afterwards.

The new young king was not a vindictive man, but he had deeply loved his father. The Declaration of Breda, issued on 4 April 1660, now included a pledge of amnesty for Charles I's enemies, with the exception of those directly involved in the king's death. Of these, Daniel Axtell's name was high on the list. His trial took place at the Old Bailey on 15 October 1660, and for me the most striking aspect of the proceedings is the respect and courtesy shown by the judges towards the prisoner. But Lord Justice Annesley, while complimenting Daniel on his painstaking research into the parliamentary precedents for removing unsatisfactory monarchs, tells him: 'Mr Axtell, I am very sorry to see you in that place, and it troubles me as much to hear you vent that for an Authority which you know yourself was no Authority.' The prosecuting counsel adds more forcefully: 'You well know that before you could do this horrid murder of the King you (and Colonel Pride) *destroyed* the Parliament.'

A procession of witnesses testifies that throughout the king's trial, Colonel Axtell encouraged his redcoats to cry 'Justice!'

'I have read some law books,' rejoins Daniel calmly, 'and I cannot find that the word Justice should be made Treason.'

The cries of 'Execution!' at the end of the king's trial are less easy to explain away and the accused's claim that he was merely a soldier acting under orders receives the identical response to the same excuse at Nuremberg three hundred years later. Reading the transcript of his trial, it is quite clear that there is more than enough genuine evidence to convict the prisoner, but the prosecution cannot resist over-egging the pudding. The odious Colonel Huncks, who has turned informer to save his own neck, testifies that Oliver Cromwell and Colonel Axtell personally tried to coerce him into signing the king's death warrant. Where did this conversation take place? In the bedroom of Major General Ireton at Westminster, an unlikely claim given that Ireton and Axtell couldn't stand each other. Another witness, formerly a soldier under his command, blurts out that Colonel Axtell once punished him for some military misdemeanour. 'My Lords, I hope you will take note of that,' comments Daniel drily.

The identity of the man who beheaded Charles I was kept so secret that even now, after three-and-a-half centuries of speculation, it is still unknown, but yet another witness swears that Daniel confided to him that the king was executed by two characters called Hewlett and Walker, who sound irresistibly like a firm of seedy solicitors. In a performance worthy of Pooh-Bah, Sir Purbeck Temple alleges that by bribing one of Daniel's soldiers, he was allowed to view the martyred king's corpse, the head of which 'smiled as perfectly as if it had been alive'.

The entry in Samuel Pepys's diary for Friday, 19 October 1660, reads: 'This morning my dining-room was finished with green serge and gilt leather, which is very handsome. Hacker and Axtell were hanged and quartered.'

If you have managed to keep company with me throughout this chapter, you will have no doubt that I have more than a little admiration for Colonel Daniel Axtell, Puritan and regicide, not only because two of my grandchildren share his genes but also because the most conspicuous aspects of his flinty and uncompromising character are his honesty, his courage and his unswerving faithfulness to the beliefs for which he fought. He died bravely at Tyburn after praying (over-optimistically, as it happens) for the conversion of King Charles II to godliness, and declaring: 'If I had a thousand lives, I could lay them all down for the Good Old Cause.'

Laughing Roundhead

A graduate student in computing, Ken Todd was my Lancaster University debating partner for such prestigious events as the Observer Mace competition. Ken had a very different approach to public speaking from mine. I wanted to sound witty and erudite beyond my years, which is probably why I adopted a style somewhere between Winston Churchill and David Frost. In contrast, Ken spoke in a flat, rapid catarrhal patter very like that of his Knotty Ash almost-namesake. I wore a dinner jacket and academic gown for debates. Ken sported his uniform of black T-shirt and black cord trousers. In fact he had several such outfits, and on Observer Mace days he invariably wore his *best* black T-shirt and black cord trousers, though of course nobody but he and I knew this.

The Observer Mace Tournament was always perilous territory for Ken and me. In my case the problem was the one defined by Dr Johnson as 'Ignorance, madam, pure ignorance', because the topics tended to require a serious knowledge of modern history and politics which I simply did not possess, and of course this was long before the days of *Wikipedia*. The problem for Ken was that Mace events were not only serious but surrounded by ceremony, and for Ken formality was always a red rag to a particularly puckish bull.

Situated in a lovely little city with a passable castle and an absolutely magnificent cathedral, Durham is the third oldest of the English universities and prides itself on being almost Oxford or Cambridge. On this Observer Mace evening, the home team had feted

DANIEL AXTEL,
Executed at Tyburn 1660

the five visiting teams with a splendid dinner preceded by a reception with the Vice Chancellor and an assortment of local worthies. At one point I found myself sipping amontillado sherry with Sir James Duff, Lord Lieutenant of the County of Durham, who looked and sounded uncannily like Peter Cook as Sir Arthur Streeb Greebling.

'Been reading things about this feller Rajiv Gandhi,' said Sir James gruffly. 'Relative of *the* Gandhi, doncha know. I've had to do with that family before now, I can tell you. Fact is, I hanged his uncle. Nice fellow.'

Dinner over, we processed formally into an impressively panelled debating chamber, gowns akimbo and preceded by the University's own mace-bearer. The motion for this evening's debate, 'This House believes that France has stabbed her allies in the back', was not a topic I knew anything about, but having been drawn sixth in the speaking order I was reasonably well able to fudge it. For Ken, speaking at number twelve, it ought to have been a doddle, but I could tell from his increasingly bored and distracted air that most of it was passing over his head. I also had a growing conviction that he had taken advantage of the hospitality part of proceedings to imbibe rather more freely that might have been wise. Finally, speaker number eleven ground to his weary conclusion and Ken rose portentously. For a long moment his jaundiced and slightly glazed eye roved over the chamber.

'Mr President, ladies and gentlemen, all this stuff about General de Gaulle is no doubt extremely interesting,' intoned Ken, with the air of one who had found it anything but, 'however I would like to introduce you to an alternative theory of history. It has always seemed to me that the actions of great men are influenced less by philosophical conviction or even political expediency than by the fact that there are essentially only two kinds of women in the world, the voluptuous, nubile women and the frigid women. For instance, at the time of the English Civil War, the Cavaliers were married to the voluptuous, nubile women while the Puritans were saddled with the frigid women. Well,' continued Ken with a belligerent glare at his mystified audience, 'has anybody here ever heard of a laughing Roundhead?'

CHAPTER 8

UNCLE ALF AND THE AMERICAN DREAM

Ask any pub quizzer what he knows about Arthur Miller and I'll guarantee that he'll tell you that Miller married Marilyn Monroe. What he may not add is that the man also wrote one of the greatest plays in the English language, a tragedy that ranks with *Hamlet* or *King Lear*. Its theme is the American Dream, the idea that a man can start out as a nobody and end up as a somebody purely on the basis of his own talent and industry. If you've seen *Death of a Salesman* you will know that its protagonist, Willy Loman, begins as a nobody and ends as a nobody, but I am sure you would have no problem giving me a list of eminent Americans from John D. Rockefeller to Bill Gates who have walked into the jungle poor and come out with diamonds. And I am equally certain that high on your list would be the name of Henry Ford. As every schoolgirl knows, Ford was the Messiah of the modern motor industry. The very fact that he decided to put the steering wheel of his Model T on the left is the reason why most of the world drives on the right. And no doubt it also led to the British Empire's stubborn decision to drive on the *wrong* side of the road. Wouldn't any imperial Briton rather die than imitate a Yank?

Millions of words have been written about the Ford phenomenon, but the man himself remains an enigma. A fervent opponent of the colour bar in an era when racism was endemic. A published anti-Semite who eagerly employed Jews because he admired their work ethic. A rabid anti-unionist and a model boss whose workers enjoyed the best pay and conditions in the world. An economist with a vision (seventy years before Thatcher) of the free market as a path to world peace and prosperity. A pacifist and a major supplier of materiél to the Allies in World War Two. An autocrat and a team builder. And this is where Uncle Alf comes into the picture.

Henry Ford started life as the son of a poor Michigan farmer and became a mogul of industry. Alfred Haselden's beginnings were even less promising. When I was a child in Wigan my parents threatened that if I didn't study, I would finish down the pit. Alfred Haselden started out down a Wigan pit and ended up as a Director of the Ford Motor Company. There must be a moral in there somewhere. Alfred was born on 26 December 1887 at Upper Morris Street, Wigan, the last of the thirteen children of Robert Haselden and Ann Sudworth. Robert was a collier whose father, another Robert, born in 1815, the year of Waterloo, had combined coal mining with the landlordship of the Lord Nelson Inn at Seneley Green, Ashton-in-Makerfield. Reputedly the handsomest couple in Wigan, Alfred's parents Robert and Ann were the king and queen of the local roller rink.

Alf left St George's Church of England School at the age of eleven and went straight down the mine. Ten years later, having already acquired a wife and a son, he was still digging coal, and the normal expectation in Edwardian Wigan was that he would carry on doing it until he succumbed to one or more of the bronchial diseases that shortened the lives of those miners who were not killed in explosions, gassed, or crushed under falling rocks. Annie Pemberton, a lass from Richmond Street – a cock-stride from the Blue Coat School in Hallgate, where I learned my tables fifty years later – was also a collier's daughter, and though she soon swapped the plebeian Annie for the more long-curtain 'Anne', hanging on to her young husband's coat-tails in his rapid rise from collier to captain of industry was to be a hard and ultimately tragic struggle. They were married at All Saints Church in 1907 and when their only son, also an Alfred, was christened at St Catherine's, who could have predicted that Young Alf would one day lead a jazz band called the Midnight Marauders in 1930s Motown and that his singer would be my lovely second cousin Marion Hart, a girl from Wigan's Darlington Street?

Rags to riches stories always sound inevitable after they have happened, but think for a moment of the heat, the filth and the grinding drudgery of hewing coal by the light of a Davy lamp in a stiflingly hot gallery little more than two feet high, then coming off shift and going home to study. Alf enrolled in night school classes at the Wigan Mining and Technical College, still a stepping stone for tens of thousands of aspiring youngsters from all over the world. By 1912 he was working at the brand new Ford plant in Manchester, first as a clerk and then as a storekeeper, with motor parts worth thousands of pounds under his control. Recognising his potential and his enormous energy his bosses sent him to study management at their plants in Toronto and Detroit, and by 1927, a year short of his thirtieth birthday, he was Ford's works manager at Asnières sur Seine near Paris. The British are notoriously bad at foreign languages but the young ex-collier from Wigan not only learned French but came to speak it fluently.

The Wigan of a hundred years ago was a challenging place to live in. Even in the early 1960s, when most of the mines and many of the factories had gone, the air was palpable on the tongue. It was even more of a challenge if you were poor. No wonder, then, that many folk with get up and go got up and went, usually to America, where the famous golden door stood open to healthy immigrants who were prepared to roll up their sleeves and graft. For some, such as my great-uncle William Taylor, who hacked a farm out of the wilderness on the shore of Vancouver Sound, the adventure met all their expectations. For others, such as my great-great-aunt Catherine Hart, whose teenage son was killed in Chicago attempting to collect a bad debt for his stepfather, horror lay in wait. Some emigrants had already tasted tragedy at home and probably felt that things could not get worse. Alf Haselden's sister Sally, already widowed in her early twenties with a baby daughter, married my great uncle Richard Hart only to lose their little son at the age of twelve months. Alf was already well-established at Ford's and he found work for Richard at the plant at Dearborn, Michigan, as he was to do for several other relatives during the next forty years.

During the years that Alf Haselden worked for Ford he would cross the Atlantic no less than seventeen times, travelling first class on the great ocean liners of the period. Two Henry Fords entrusted him with the key tasks of sourcing and purchasing property, not only for a new factory at Poissy but also for the plant in Essex which was to play such a key role in the Allied resistance to Hitler's ambitions in World War Two. And it was narrowly ahead of the Nazi invasion of France that Alf returned to England to take direct control of Dagenham. Its contribution to the war effort was indispensable, turning out 13,000 tracked Universal Carriers, 250,000 V8 engines and 185,000 complete military vehicles.

Alf was also responsible for the plant in Manchester which produced no less than 30,000 of the supercharged 27-litre Rolls-Royce Merlin V12 engines that powered the Lancaster, Mosquito, Hurricane and Spitfire. Both factories were prime targets for the Luftwaffe and Alf's finances never quite recovered either from the direct hit that destroyed the family home in Hornchurch, or, for that matter, from the expensive lifestyles of a three-times-married son and a divorced daughter with a taste for fast planes and faster Greek aristocrats. Handsome, fair-haired Alf Junior, by now also a Ford executive, fared almost as badly as the house when the impact of an exploding bomb drove his head through the windscreen of his car. Emergency treatment amidst the wreckage prevented his bleeding to death from a punctured jugular vein, but he was left with some permanent paralysis down one side of his body.

Everyone, including Lord Beaverbrook, Winston Churchill's Minister of Supply, agreed that the contributions of the Ford Company and of Alfred Haselden to the downfall of Adolf Hitler had been outstanding, and as the war drew to its close the paperwork was already prepared that would have led to Mr Haselden's kneeling before King George VI and arising a moment later as Sir Alfred. It was not to be. In his rise to industrial greatness, Alf had left more than his pick and shovel behind in Lancashire, and the Whitehall mandarins who draw up honours lists are notoriously sensitive to the slightest scent of scandal. The following brief article appeared in the *Blackpool Evening Gazette* of 27 January 1945:

SEA MYSTERY NOT SOLVED

A mystery of the sea was left unsolved at a Blackpool inquest last night on Mrs Anne Haselden aged 54 of Lansdowne Mansions, Didsbury, Manchester, whose body was found left by the tide on the sands opposite Red Bank Road on Wednesday morning. Mr Alfred Haselden, a works manager, said his wife had been a sick woman for many years and the doctor advised her to go to Blackpool where she had been for about three weeks. Although she had been depressed she had never threatened to take her life. The proprietress of an Hotel on North Promenade where Mrs Haselden had been staying said that Mrs Haselden once asked her 'what did she think was an easy way out' but witnesses did not take her remark seriously. On bringing a cup of tea to her bedroom a maid found the bed empty. The front door was later found to be unbarred. The Deputy Coroner, Mr AL Ashton, entered a verdict of 'Found Drowned' and said he could not speculate on the condition of her mind or how she got into the water.

In keeping with the etiquette of his profession, the Deputy Coroner was being scrupulous in refusing to speculate on the basis of the slender evidence available, but of course there were those both inside and outside the family who did speculate and come to their own conclusions. Our family tradition is that a lonely, ailing and neglected woman, whose husband had compelling interests elsewhere, deliberately walked into the near-freezing waters of the Irish Sea on that bleak January morning. What were those compelling interests? The main one, of course had been Alf's war work at Ford. The other was Peggy Miller.

Slim, dark-haired Margaret Winifred Miller was Alfred Haselden's personal secretary at the Ford aircraft engine factory in Manchester.

Pefkos/ Bigstock

Alf married her at the Manchester register office a year after Annie's death, when he was sixty and she was little more than half his age. Now the war was over, Alf was back to managing Dagenham through the launch of the new generation of American-styled Zodiacs, Zephyrs and Consuls which were about to sweep the British market. In my photograph his three-year-old daughter Patricia sits on the bonnet of a 1952 Ford Zephyr with her proud father standing on one side and her  forty-four-year-old half-brother Alf Junior on the other.

In 1955, Alf and Peggy retired to their rural villa in Northern Ireland, but their adventures were not yet over. On 19 December 1962, a week before Alf's seventy-fifth birthday, they set sail from Southampton on the Greek liner *Lakonia* for an eleven-day Christmas cruise to Madeira and the Canary Islands. Launched in 1929, the *Lakonia* had tramped around the Far East followed by six hard years as a troop carrier in World War Two, and by the early 1960s she was feeling all of her thirty-three years. She had just undergone a partial overhaul, but in spite of all her gleaming new paint she was no more than a whited sepulchre, an image that was soon to take on a grisly aptness. The glossy brochure showed the two swimming pools, the tennis courts, the nightclub, the cinema, the crystal chandeliers and the marble staircases, but beneath the glittering art deco surface were symptoms of age and decay untouched by the cosmetic refit.

From the beginning of the voyage there were numerous complaints about the erratic electrical heating system. Some cabins were cold, others unbearably stuffy. On the fourth evening, about 180 miles north of Madeira, a perspiring passenger laid a hand on the bulkhead between her cabin and the ship's beauty salon and it was blisteringly hot to the touch. Opening the salon door, a steward found the room ablaze. There was no sprinkler system and the fire extinguishers proved ineffective. Peggy recalled later that the ship's defective alarm system tinkled so feebly that it sounded like someone calling the waiter to ask for tea.

The flames spread rapidly toward the passenger cabins and the public areas of the vessel. Many of the passengers, jiving at the Tropical Tramps' Ball, knew nothing of the emergency until the band stopped playing as smoke began to billow into the ballroom. In a shouting, gesticulating babel of conflicting orders, Greek officers tried to herd dazed passengers, some in pyjamas and others still in fancy dress or evening wear, into the main dining room, below decks and directly in the path of the fire, while cruise director George Herbert more sensibly ushered them in the other direction towards the boat deck.

There were many individual examples of heroism. Crew members risked their own lives on the burning accommodation decks to save passengers who had been asleep when the fire started. A steward and a swimming pool attendant lowered themselves on ropes to pull trapped people out through portholes. The medical officer Dr O'Riordan first rescued the ship's chaplain then shrugged off his own life jacket and gave it to a woman who was struggling in the water. He was not seen alive again. Antonios Kalogridis, the *Lakonia*'s radio officer, remained at his post, sending SOS messages until driven out by the flames. Captain Zarbis seemed to have lost control of his crew and shortly before one o'clock in the morning it was the Purser who gave the order to abandon ship.

For those passengers who were able to reach their lifeboat stations, escape ought to have been a matter of course, but here again chaos reigned. Some boats were already aflame. In other cases, the chains had rusted into the davits and the boat either refused to move or hung vertically from one end, spilling its occupants into the sea. The drain holes of many of the boats were without plugs, so passengers had to bail constantly to keep them afloat.

Rocked by violent explosions, the *Lakonia* continued to burn fiercely. When all the viable lifeboats, some only half full, had been launched, there were still over a hundred people left on board, crammed into the glass-enclosed Agora shopping centre at the stern of the ship, with the flames closing in on them. Some of the more able-bodied managed to descend on swinging rope ladders, but others jumped overboard, struck the side of the ship on the way down, and were dead or unconscious before they hit the water. Belatedly, someone thought of lowering the port and starboard gangways, and the remaining passengers were able to walk calmly down them in single file into the sea.

At 3.30 a.m., four hours after the first distress call, the rescue ships began to arrive but, with so many survivors in the water, their approach to the burning liner had to be cautious and there was the constant risk that the tons of fuel oil aboard the *Lakonia* might explode. At dawn, RAF and USAAF aircraft from Gibraltar and the Azores patrolled the area dropping life rafts and flares to guide rescuers to the survivors who were now dispersed over three miles of ocean. A boat was despatched from the liner *Charlesville* shortly after daybreak to rescue Captain Zarbis, who had been spotted pacing the decks of the still-burning ship. He was the last person to leave the *Lakonia* alive.

On Christmas Eve, crewmen from the British aircraft carrier *HMS Centaur* boarded the charred and smoking hulk to recover the bodies of those who had died in the blaze. Seventeen-year-old Gordon Holme recalled: 'Even before we could clearly see the *Lakonia* there was a strong smell of smoke and oil in the air. Our boats bobbed about in the fast running, heavy swell and we looked on in dismay at the white faces of the victims who seemed to stare back at us. It was hard to believe that only a few hours before they had been going about their crew duties or enjoying themselves at a dance. On Christmas Day we arrived at Gibraltar and started the gruesome task of lowering the bodies on mesh cradles down to a floating pontoon from the dockyard. Christmas dinner was being served in our dining hall, but there were not many takers. It was the only Christmas Day in my life when I didn't sit down and enjoy the festivities.'

Tugs took the *Lakonia* in tow towards Gibraltar. Her superstructure had partially collapsed amidships, and the bridge and aft decks had caved in. There were holes blasted near the bow, and she was listing ten degrees to starboard. At about 2 p.m. on December 29, 250 miles west of Gibraltar, she rolled over on to her starboard side and sank stern-first in only three minutes.

One hundred and twenty-eight people died in the *Lakonia* disaster, of whom ninety-five were passengers and thirty-three crew members. Only fifty-three people died in the fire. The rest succumbed to exposure, drowning and injuries sustained while diving overboard. In the end, just over half of the *Lakonia*'s lifeboats had made it safely away from the burning ship and in one of them were Alfred and Peggy Haselden. Although Alf was long-retired it was clear that his former employers still thought the world of him and the Ford Motor Company of England despatched a private aircraft to bring them home to Ireland. Alf never fully recovered from the *Lakonia* experience and died in Dublin less than two years later. He had maintained affectionate ties with his sister Sally in Michigan and her granddaughter Madeline recalls: 'His daughter Pat and I were exactly the same age. They would all come to Detroit to visit grandma and we would go downtown to Hudson's where Uncle Alf would have Pat and me fitted out like twins in matching outfits.'

Pat and Madeline now have grandchildren of their own.

That Was Jennifer Moss

I once went to a party at the home of a *Coronation Street* star. She was still in her teens and lived with her parents in a big house on Wigan Road in Standish and she was called Jennifer Moss. 'Jennifer who?' I hear you ask, but Jenny, who joined the series as Lucille Hewitt in 1960, was as famous in those early Corrie days as Ena Sharples and, with her snub nose, gamine curls and sparkling eyes she was a lot prettier. I didn't know her well. What am I saying? I didn't know her at all, but she'd attended Wigan Girls' High School with my girlfriend Audrey and I suppose that must have been the connection. Jenny continued acting in the Street until 1973, when her alcoholism got the better of her. She went through four failed marriages before finally finding peace with a fifth husband and dying in 2006 at the age of sixty-one.

Few, if any, of the intellectual circles Val and I have moved in over the years (and what a disturbing metaphor for life those circles are) have included folk with a good word for Corrie. They don't actually watch it, you understand, but they do occasionally catch an episode by accident, as it were, out of the corner of the eye, perhaps while doing the ironing, restoring an antique corner cupboard or re-reading Schopenhauer's biggest hits, and on this admittedly tenuous basis they all agree that it's rubbish. The storylines are contrived (unlike *Doctor Who, Shrek* or *Romeo and Juliet*, for instance) and the acting wooden and unconvincing.

If I'm busy at my favourite conversational occupation of gilding a nugget of truth, I enjoy informing my loftily intellectual friends that I became a *Coronation Street* addict when I watched the first episode in 1960 and have remained an unswerving devotee right up to the present day. It isn't quite true, of course. During three of those years I was at university, largely preoccupied with what W. S. Gilbert called 'beer and beauty', not to mention my other passions for debating and vintage cars. For the first three years of our marriage Val and I didn't even possess a TV set and throughout much of the 1970s our evenings were largely occupied with amdram and music-making. Then, belatedly

Jennifer Moss

and thankfully, when we had almost given up hope, there was child-rearing followed by almost twenty years abroad in wild and lawless parts of Latin America, Africa and Asia where even the writ of Granada Television didn't run.

During home leave and the intervals between doing this and that, we did of course watch many individual episodes of *Coronation Street*, but the 2010 rash of documentaries for the fiftieth anniversary of the show revealed that we had missed whole swathes of plot. The fiftieth anniversary! What an opportunity for our current circle of intelligentsia (hardly bigger than a hula hoop these days) to tut and shake their heads over the blatant sensationalism of that train crash which was quite clearly aimed at stealing the soap awards back from *EastEnders*. The same lofty criticisms as ever came trotting out but, I notice, with an interesting variation: the acting is now not just wooden, it is far below the standard of those first, grainy, gritty, black and white episodes. But if they would only take the trouble to abandon Schopenhauer for a moment, and sit down to *watch* an early episode, our critical friends might even have to abandon that opinion.

The very first episode of *Coronation Street* is a fascinating historical document because in all kinds of ways it was breaking new ground, not only in British but also in world television. But most of the performances, even those of Violet Carson as Ena and Pat Phoenix as Elsie Tanner, still have a touch of the Little Theatre about them which has now been absent from Corrie since the wonderful, but blatantly stagy John Savident retired from hamming it up behind the bacon counter.

Frankly, my dears, many of today's Corrie cast could act most of their predecessors not only off the set, but down the Street and into the job centre as well. Comparisons, as Constable Dogberry justly observed, are odorous, and it might seem difficult to pick one name out of a stellar cast, but if young Craig Gazely, who played the eccentric Graeme Proctor a year or four ago, was not put on this earth expressly to play Trinculo, Feste, Touchstone and Launcelot Gobbo, I'll eat my cap and bells.

Watch that first episode of Corrie. It still stands up pretty well despite my reservation about the staginess of some of the acting, and veterans Jack Howarth and Doris Speed even escape that stricture. And if you don't nip out to make the tea you won't miss a bright cheeky little voice just off camera calling Elsie a silly old cow. That was Jennifer Moss.

CHAPTER 9

MADAME TEAPOT TAKES DRASTIC MEASURES

Introducing La Belle France to Le Chip Butty is one of Wigan's lesser-known contributions to the *entente cordiale*.

Madame Teapot was one of the more intriguing members of the cast of characters who enlivened my time as a pupil at Wigan Grammar School. For most of the rest, 'intriguing' would have been an inappropriate description. Ralph Downing, for example, was exuberant, often entertaining and occasionally terrifying, but he was not intriguing. You felt instinctively that you knew where you were with him: on safe ground if you behaved yourself and struck by lightning if you didn't. But Madame Teapot was an enigma. To begin with there was the matter of her surname which was not of course Teapot but Tison, pronounced 'Teeson' in the French manner, though she also answered, apparently happily, to 'Mrs Tyson'. So was she English or was she French? A petite, shapely, dark-eyed woman in her early fifties, toujours soignée, her hair always in an immaculate pleat, she certainly looked thoroughly Gallic. She even had a couple of well-groomed, well-behaved poodles who waited for her in the car while she was teaching and greeted her enthusiastically when she returned. From early childhood I have been attracted or repelled by voices and hers was one of the most attractive voices I had ever heard, a deepish contralto with clear, rounded vowels and, in English, the cut-glass consonants of Roedean or Cheltenham Ladies' College. On good authority, her spoken French was as impeccable as her English and this was clearly the basis of her part-time role at WGS, rather than the grind of written proses and translations which seemed to dominate the public examination syllabuses of those days.

Then, of course, there was the even more intriguing fact that Madame Tison was one of the few women, and certainly the most enduring and the most attractive woman, on the WGS staff. Ladies tended to come and go, usually to fill temporary vacancies, but Madame Tison, like

Hesdin: Le Petit Café   *annaspeirs/Bigstock*

Tennyson's brook, seemed to go on forever. Odder still, in a school in which playing-up the staff was a time-honoured sport, she never had to raise her voice and she appeared to have absolutely no discipline problems. During one of our individual sessions during my final year at school when I was in the 'scholarship' sixth form I asked her about this.

'Ah! But it wasn't always so. When I joined the school just after the War the barbarians gave me a very rough time. And of course one is expected to sink or swim on one's own merits. If I had gone crying to the headmaster it would have confirmed the chauvinists in their predictable prejudices.'

111

'So what did you do?'

'I had a particularly rowdy fifth-form class, so I shifted their next lesson to the classroom at the top of the tower, the one nobody likes to use because it's such a wearisome climb to get up there, the great advantage being that there are also no witnesses if one has decided on drastic measures.'

'Drastic?'

'Ecoutes-moi. I set them a piece of written work and I warned them that if anybody misbehaved or even spoke until the bell went for the end of the lesson there would be unpleasant consequences.'

'And then?'

'Of course the class clown, the usual ringleader, was the first one to break the silence. So I hit him.'

'You hit him?'

'Yes. I know exactly how to hit people. I can hit them very painfully in ways that leave no marks.'

'And it worked?'

'As you see. I was a young widow and I needed the job. Reputations can be made very quickly if one is determined or desperate and I was both.'

This was even more intriguing. A pretty, petite young widow who was expert in inflicting pain? Even in those pre-PC days these were not skills routinely taught at the Sorbonne or at English teacher training colleges.

As with most of our handful of interactions during the several years in which I knew her, first as a student and later as a colleague, I did not share this conversation with any of my contemporaries, one or two of whom had teased me about my one-to-one classes with what they chose to call my French mistress.

'Madame is old enough to be my mother,' I told them stiffly.

'Quite true but she's also a cracker.'

'Do you really think so?'

'Yes I do and so do you.'

Though I came to know her rather better than most of my contemporaries, Madame Tison was not of course pally with her pupils. Teachers weren't in those days. She similarly seemed to keep her distance from the male staff, floating in elegantly to take her classes and then floating off with her poodles rather than joining in any of the staffroom chat. Even so, she was invariably polite and pleasant to all of us, with one perennial, or annual, exception: the German assistant, whom she cut dead. The year I returned from Lancaster University to teach at WGS the assistant was a pleasant, quietly spoken girl who was puzzled and distressed that the only other female on the staff would not speak to her or even acknowledge her existence. I felt sorry for Fraulein Löffler, who was gentle, doe-like and had nice legs, so acting on my usual principles of 'in for a pfennig, in for a mark' and 'where Engels feared to tread', I tackled Madame Tison about the problem. She regarded me sombrely but paid me the supreme compliment of not telling me to go and boil my head.

'John, the Germans shot my husband. And I saw many, many other unspeakable things done by the Master Race to the people of my adopted country. No, I will not speak to any of them. And if I thought it would prevent such things happening again I would strangle their babies.'

Madame Tison's late husband's family still lived at Hesdin in the Pas de Calais, and I suppose it was this continuing link which caused the school to choose that location in 1962 for its annual Scout camp. My friend James Bradshaw and I were not Scouts, but there were a couple of spare places and we were allowed to join in provided that we faithfully practised our dibs and dobs and suitably togged ourselves up in the shirts, shorts, bandanas, woggles and so on, favoured by the Baden Powellite fraternity. One of my memories of this trip is that, in spite of a complete absence of insignia of rank, or the usual badges awarded for tracking, arson, jam-making or removing wolf cubs from horses' hooves, Jim was invariably hailed by the local populace as Le Chef, by which they meant 'The Boss' rather than 'The Cook'. The ghosts of Napoleon and Nelson may scoff, but this should be an object lesson to us all in the managerial advantage of being blond, six-feet-two, and handsome with it.

Hesdin, close to the Flanders border, was the birthplace in 1697 of the Abbé Prévost, who, in spite of his clerical title, was intermittently a soldier and the author of such worldly works as *Manon Lescaut*. During his time in England he even converted to Anglicanism though he later apologised nicely to the Pope, who received him back into the Roman Catholic Church. Not much seemed to have happened in Hesdin since then, but we found it a pleasant introduction to the culture of the Continong.

We camped in a forest close to the town and made occasional excursions to sights such as the New Menin Gate, a stupendous and moving monument to the First World War dead. Later that day we stood in well-tended cemeteries where identical gravestones stretched to the far horizon in surrealistically converging parallel lines. Kneeling to read the inscriptions from 1918 I saw that among both the British and the German dead there were many men in their late thirties and forties and many others of my own age and even younger, exhausted enemies scraping their respective conscript barrels. On another day Jim dragged me at breakneck speed round the sights of Paris, oblivious to my protest that we were 'not bloody Americans, you know'.

Hesdin had two attractions which were not normally available to schoolboys in 1960s Wigan, and a rather surprising third which was. As long as we didn't overdo it, the staff in charge of the trip turned a blind eye to our evening visits to a pavement café in the Place d'Armes where I drank my first ever glasses of vin blanc. (I really fancied the vin rouge but for some reason that seemed a sinful step too far). The boulangerie close to the café sold the most delicious long French loaves, the kind of bread which tastes and smells so good that it can be devoured without butter. And, wonder of wonders, in the middle of the square there was a fish and chip stall which was equal or superior to any at home. Mischievously, somebody asked the proprietor for 'un chip butty, s'il vous plait'.

'Comment?'

'Un chip butty, monsieur.'

'Qu'est que c'est?'

'Vous avez du pain. Et vous mettez des pommes frites. Et enfin vous mettez encore du pain. Voilá un chip butty!'

From that moment Le Chip Butty was officially on the menu of the Hesdin fish and chip establishment. Before starting to write this chapter I looked at the official Hesdin website. In the interest of promoting tourism, the Town Council has gone to the trouble of producing an alternative version in perfect English which, unlike so many of its kind, has clearly been composed by a native speaker. So far I haven't actually found a reference to Le Chip Butty, but I bet it's there somewhere, an enduring monument to the Hesdin-Wigan *entente cordiale*.

Madame Tison did not of course accompany us on our excursion to the Pas de Calais. Though as far as both the staff and students were concerned she would no doubt have been very welcome, it was difficult to imagine her in the context of a Scout camp in her elegantly tailored two-piece, the small poodles swirling excitedly round her neat mid-heel court shoes with their buttoned ankle-straps. Probably, too, the memories of Hesdin and the young husband she had lost would still have been too painful less than twenty years after the War. But we were reminded of her all the same when we were greeted on arrival by her husband's uncle. An erect, handsome, white-haired figure in his seventies, immaculate in a crisply tailored linen suit, Monsieur Tison was the spit and image of one of the stars of Vicente Minelli's hit movie *Gigi*, and when he opened his mouth the resemblance was complete. 'Maurice Chevalier!' we muttered, mesmerised and, privately at least, Monsieur Tison became 'Maurice' from that moment. He was one of those adults who, without making the slightest concession to trendiness, have the enviable ability to establish an immediate rapport with the young. As he squired us around the Hôtel de Ville, Monsieur Tison remarked: 'Wigan, I regret to admit that I 'ave nevair been thair, but London! Mon dieu, what a wonderful city!'

'Do you know London well, Sir?'

'Thair was a time when I knew eet vairy well but of course that was before the War.'

'So you haven't visited England since 1939?'

'1939! Non, non. I meant the FIRST war. I was last in London in nineteen hundred and seven. Tell me, do they still 'ave the 'ansome cabs?'

I recounted this conversation to Madame Tison on our return to Wigan and she smiled. 'Yes. He is quite a character. And speaking of 1907, his car is just about that vintage. Think of the car in the *Genevieve* film.'

'That was a 1904 Darracq.'

'Vraiment? You will know much more about these things than I.

But that is the sort of thing Uncle still drives. The hood is long gone, the lights don't work and the brakes are hit and miss, but he piles his shotguns and fishing rods in the back and trundles off along the farm tracks into the countryside. He is a popular character and has held important posts in local government. He keeps off the real roads so the gendarmes don't bother him.'

'We all liked him.'

'I'm sure you did. He is an individual. Something of an eccentric.'

'It's the same with teachers. Mr Skirrow, for instance...'

'We will not continue this line of conversation.'

'Non, Madame. D'accord.'

In spite of Jim Bradshaw's faux local reputation as a leader of youth, our real Senior Scout was an upper-sixth-former named Mason whom we were encouraged to address as 'Bal'. This, it transpired, was short for 'Baloo', because for some arcane reason known only to their Craft it is the custom for senior Boy Scouts and Girl Guides to adopt names from Kipling's *Jungle Book*. Whatever the reason, 'Baloo the Bear' seemed a very appropriate identity for Mason, who, large, beefy and kindly, ruled us with a light touch, though with his massive physique he could have overpowered any three with one hand tied behind his back. There was in fact one moment when Bal's mighty shoulders threatened to wipe out the whole troop but this was entirely unintentional.

After Monsieur Tison had shown us around the lower reaches of the Hôtel de Ville, he encouraged us to climb its impressive tower and enjoy the view from the top. This idea appealed and we set off enthusiastically. We were young and fit so the first two-thirds, involving narrow stone staircases, were accomplished easily. Then we emerged into the high chamber which housed the huge town clock and its carillon. Suddenly there was no more staircase. Instead there was a narrow wooden ladder of exactly the kind used by window cleaners at home. This led up at an angle of forty-five degrees to a small square plank platform in the right angle of two of the walls at roughly half the fifty-foot height of the bell chamber. From this platform an identical ladder at the opposite forty-five-degree angle from the first led up to a tiny doorway which gave access to the roof. I do not like heights but there was obviously no way I could back out of this one and still maintain face, though in fact

I think most of us were rather daunted by the prospect of this exposed climb. As befitted his senior role, Bal Mason was the first to grasp the figurative nettle and the actual ladder. I made an instant decision that if I was going to do this thing at all I would rather be next in line behind a trusty Leader than be sandwiched between a couple of fellow ditherers, so I followed him on to the ladder which was soon thrumming to the footsteps of a couple of dozen youths, and flexing rather alarmingly.

'Look up, lads! Don't look down.'

It was good advice, but all the same I was acutely conscious of the yawning gulf opening up to my left and I had to work hard at relaxing my spasmodic white-knuckled clutching at the side rails of the ladder so I could continue moving onwards and upwards. The oddest part of the climb was the ascent of the second ladder when, in spite of Bal's sensible exhortations, I looked down through the rungs and saw a row of white faces peering up at me. The two ladders were of course at right angles to each other. The noise of clattering feet and thrumming wood and the clouds of dust almost overwhelmed the senses, and the sheer strangeness of the opposed angles threatened to confuse the perception of up, down and sideways, so it was with some relief that I looked up again and saw that we had reached the trapdoor on to the roof. Coming down, I had already decided, I would, like Sir Thomas More, shift for myself. The herd could clatter away first and I would return by gentler stages.

But before I could come *down* from the roof, I had to get *on to* the roof and I couldn't help noticing that progress had stopped. Like Houston in another context we had a problem, and the problem was Bal. As he attempted to heave himself off the last rungs of the ladder and on to the leads, his mighty shoulders had stuck fast in the aperture of the trapdoor. Twenty-four of us hung in space like a human totem pole or a flying buttress full of worried gargoyles. Reversing would have been complicated and potentially dangerous. What am I saying? Everything up to this point had already been dangerous. Jim was literally hard on my heels. Bal's size thirteen boots were within inches of my nose. He heaved again and the rung on which he stood bent like the one string fiddle in the *Ballad of Eskimo Nell*. He stamped to give himself more purchase. The rung flexed alarmingly and the ladder shuddered along its length, resounding in the confines of the bell chamber like a massive tea-chest bass. A chorus of moans arose dismally from the abyss. Then pop! Bal shot upwards on to the roof like a portly genie or a cork from an oversized bottle and the rest of us followed.

I don't remember a great deal about the view from the tower of the Hôtel de Ville, except that it gave us a bird's eye view of the market stalls in the Place d'Armes. Someone mentioned Galileo's experiment of dropping both a musket ball and a cannon ditto from the Leaning Tower of Pisa, and suggested that if we released a five centime coin the acceleration from this altitude would allow it to pierce one of the canvas awnings.

'Don't even think about it,' growled Bal, his face still brick-red from exertion.

'It's been an interesting morning, but if I ever look like climbing anything again, please kill me first,' I muttered to Jim when we finally reached terra firma.

I mentioned earlier that we camped in a forest just outside Hesdin, and in keeping with the general laissez-faire ambience of the trip we were allowed to select our own pitches within a certain radius of the camp fire and the stores bell-tent, so Jim and I had chosen a gently sloping site and set about erecting our tent. It had been used by his father on his own schoolboy camping trips and as Mr Bradshaw was then about sixty it was something of an antique, a heavy canvas First World War army ridge tent which caused some mirth among our scouting colleagues, all of whom seemed to have the latest lightweight models. I had brought an airbed with me but I felt that it would have been infra dig to allow Jim to sleep on the ground while I kipped in luxury, so I decided on the spot that we would use it turn and turn about. Bal Mason, as Senior Scout, had first pick of potential pitches and chose a position in a long shallow depression in the forest floor where, he said, his dome tent would be snugly protected from the lashings of wind and rain. In the event it had seemed to be an unnecessary precaution because all week the weather had been ideal for camping, sunny, cloudless, warm but not too hot.

It was our last evening in France. Tomorrow, early, we would strike camp, load the tents and baggage into the Botts of Pemberton 'chara' rented for the week along with Alan its genial driver, and take the road to Calais and Wigan. So, after supper, having more or less packed our rucksacks and cases, we seniors strolled off for a last boisson in the Place d'Armes.

'I don't fancy the wine tonight.'

'Funnily enough neither do I.'

'I think I might have cold a beer. Or even a lemonade.'

'Blasphemy!'

'Not really. It's too hot and sticky for alcohol. I'm sweating cobs already from the walk.'

When we left the café at about ten o'clock, the summer sky was still quite light, but only a few glimmers penetrated the canopy of trees as we trudged back through the forest towards camp. On every other evening we would have been pulling on jackets and sweaters by this time, but tonight the heat and humidity, rather than dissipating, seemed to be building in intensity. There was not a breath of wind and the spicy scents of leaf mould and fungus were overpowering. An almost tangible feeling of tension seemed to affect the whole group.

Suddenly sheet lightning illuminated the black trunks of the trees and the straggling line of walkers with flickering blue light. A crash of thunder. Wind, lashing the leaves and bending the saplings. And then, without a word or a cry, a figure was breaking ranks and plunging noisily through the woods to the right of the track, and I remember thinking in that split second that it was nothing short of miraculous that he did not injure himself by crashing headlong into a tree trunk or impaling himself on a dead branch. I doubt if most of us had a clue as to what was happening. But Bal Mason did. 'It's a fit,' he snapped tersely as he plunged off in pursuit of the fugitive. When the rest of us had caught up he was sitting with his arms around the petit mal sufferer and the incident was more or less over. But not the storm.

By the time we reached camp the voice of the wind had risen to a shriek and the rain was coming down in stair rods. Jim and I dived into our old ridge tent and prepared to batten down the hatches. We were pleased to see by the light of an electric torch that so far no water was coming through the canvas, but the slight slope of the ground meant that it was seeping under one of the gable walls and on to the groundsheet. My raincoat (it was never quite the same again) solved that one, and the good news was that it was my turn for the airbed. It was not a particularly restful night. In addition to the screaming of the storm there were the confused sounds outside the tent of voices in various treble and bass keys. Round about midnight one of the harassed staff members arrived to present us with a soggy second former who looked rather like a bedraggled piglet, and eventually we settled down in the small hours and dropped off to sleep.

We crawled out sleepily at something past seven in the morning to a scene of dripping devastation, and had the last laugh on our tent's detractors. Breakfast was cooked and served in a splendid medieval barn belonging to a friendly farmer, and it turned out that apart from our *ménage à trois* the whole troop had spent most of the night there. In addition to ours there were exactly two other tents still standing: the stores 'bell' which was almost as venerable as ours, and Bal Mason's spanking new tent. You may remember that Bal had pitched it in a long, shallow depression in the forest floor, where he said it would be protected from the lashings of wind and rain. What he had failed to realise was that his sleepy hollow was part of a storm drain. All that was visible of Bal's safe house above the swirling brown water was the top six inches of its dome.

As a teacher in later years I often noticed how some of my pupils seemed to have put on an extra spurt of growth during the vacations. After registration on the first morning back at school I took the lower sixth register to the secretary in the school office and found her in conversation with my French teacher.

'Me voici de retour de Hesdin, Madame.'

Madame Tison regarded me with a faint smile then, to my great surprise, took one of my hands in both of hers.

'This boy is becoming a man,' she murmured quietly to Mrs Lyons. 'You can tell it from his hands.'

'Careful, Madame, you'll be making him blush.'

Another faint smile. 'I think not.'

I have remembered this small incident with considerable pleasure for almost fifty years, but neither then nor now did I exaggerate its significance and of course I would not have dreamed of sharing it with my schoolmates. It could only have happened with another female member of staff present and (unfortunately) it would never have occurred in one of our one-to-one sessions. There was nothing flirtatious about it. It was simply charming and very French.

Les Soucis De Quasimodo

A friend of Oscar Wilde's had just produced a particularly witty bon mot.

'Oh, how I wish I'd said that!' exclaimed Oscar.

'You will, Oscar, you will,' was the smiling reply.

All I can plead in my own defence is that when my university debating colleague Ken Todd first told the following story, it was less than a tenth of the current length. Like Pinocchio's nose, it has grown over the intervening forty-something years.

Quasimodo had been worried about the publicity. He enjoyed his work and, indeed, anything at all to do with campanology, and he was blissfully happy in his new life with Esmeralda, though, with the impending patter of tiny hunchbacks, their little apartment in the bell tower high above the Ile de la Cité was certainly going to feel a bit cramped. What worried him most was the thought that the even tenor of their life (even when worried, Quasimodo relished a pun) might be disturbed by prying visitors or, even worse, the paparazzi.

It had all started with the novel. And it had, of course, been just that: a novel. Quasimodo often smiled to himself when he thought of that tragic and entirely fictional ending, with him and Esmeralda embracing in their common grave. Then there had been the film of the book, starring Mr Laughton, whose Hollywood good looks, Quasimodo humbly believed, had been too conventionally handsome for the role.

Then there had been the book of the film for those readers who couldn't read French or, if they could, would certainly have struggled with M. Hugo's polysyllables and gothic flights of fancy. Then the radio and TV interviews and the articles in the glossy illustrated magazines (Quasimodo always insisted on being photographed on his good side) such as *Allo, Elle,* and, of course, *Bell.*

Suddenly, from being an obscure functionary, the bell-ringer found himself the most famous hunchback in Paris... in France... in the whole world. And, truth to tell, he was surprised to discover that he enjoyed it. People made pilgrimages to see him at work, not only from all over France but from every conceivable country on the face of the earth.

As I've already mentioned, the only real drawback to all this adulation was the lack of room to swing a cat. Not that Quasimodo literally wanted to swing a cat. Having himself suffered a great deal of unkindness in his earlier life, he was always extremely tender towards the underdogs, and indeed, undercats of this world. In point of fact, he and Esmeralda had a much-loved ginger tom called Robert le Majeur, who had his own tale, though it doesn't come into the present story. No, Quasimodo didn't want to swing a cat, but as the Cathedral's senior campanologist he most emphatically did need room to swing a bell, and a very large bell at that. The bell in question was Emmanuel, le Grand Bourdon de Nôtre Dame, greatest of the Cathedral's mighty peal, weighing all of thirteen tonnes. Naturally, Quasimodo was a past master of the art of change ringing with the usual apparatus of ropes and sliders, but his particular party piece was to ring his beloved Emmanuel using only the strength of his mighty arms. All of which brings us to the tragic incident of the American in Paris.

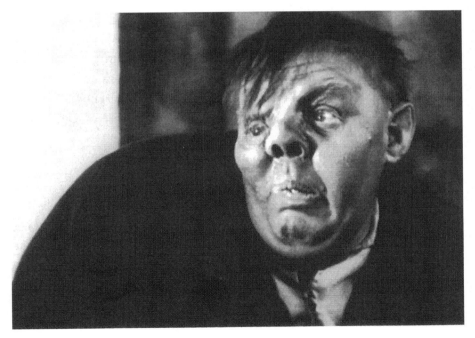

It was a bright, sunny spring day with the plane trees along the rive of the Seine bursting into joyous leaf. The bell chamber was full of visitors all eager to see Quasimodo perform, and he was determined not to disappoint them. He flexed his bulging biceps, grasped the great bell's bronze lip and applied his gargantuan strength. For a moment Emmanuel's dead weight continued to hang plumb, then centimetre by centimetre he swung on his axis until he was balanced at a forty-five-degree angle, sustained only by the hunchback's straining sinews. Then suddenly Quasimodo leapt clear as the bell swung back to the perpendicular with a deep, satisfying BOOOM!

It was an amazing feat and the assembled crowd of tourists burst into spontaneous applause. But one young American had watched the bell-ringer's virtuoso performance with particular fascination, and as Quasimodo signed his autograph book with the practised flourish of the celebrity campanologist, he whispered in awed tones: 'Gee, Mr Modo, I'd just lurve to do that. Do you think I could?'

'I very much doubt it. It's extremely dangerous. How do you think the non-photogenic side of my face got to be like this?'

'Aw gee, Mr Modo, I carry a stack of insurance. Just let me have a go!'

'Very well, but on your head be it. Literally, I rather fear.'

To cut a lengthening story short, the young American did indeed try to replicate Quasimodo's extraordinary feat, but unfortunately he failed to leap clear quickly enough. To the horror and dismay of all present the edge of the great bell struck him a thirteen-tonne hammer blow and he flew straight out between the louvres of the bell chamber and fell a hundred metres to the cobblestones below.

By the time Quasimodo and the shocked tourists had straggled down the tortuous spiral staircase to ground level, a crowd had gathered round the shattered body of the young American, and a puzzled gendarme was reaching for his notebook.

'Can anybody identify this man?'

Gazing down at the pathetic corpse, Quasimodo murmured sadly 'Non, monsieur l'agent… His face just doesn't ring a bell.'

CHAPTER 10

WINNIE AND WILSON

As curious teenagers, my wife Val and her sister Margaret managed to ferret out half of this story from their reluctant Aunt. Fifty years later I discovered the surprising conclusion out there in cyber-space.

Q: What was the longest pass in the history of Rugby League?
A: Ashton to Boston, three thousand miles.

The story I am about to tell involves an even longer pass, which started in Pemberton with a Victorian collier's youngest son, bounced through Quebec and the Carolinas, bounced again in Louisiana, and goes bounding on to the present day.

'We called him Will-Double-Dot because that was always how he signed himself,' recalled Avril Fishwick.

I never met my wife Val's maternal grandfather who died in 1955, but his was a name which cropped up in unexpected places. One Thursday evening after rehearsal, Alec Brown, my colleague in the Parish Church choir and a senior executive with the Salford City Development Corporation, mentioned over a welcome pint of Flowers' bitter in the Grand Hotel that he owed much to the managing clerk of a local firm of solicitors, Ackerley, Heaton and Pigot, a shrewd and honest investment counsellor who had put him on to many a 'good thing'.

'That man was a genius,' said Alec. 'If there were any justice in the world they would have made him a partner.'

'They did,' I told him, relishing his surprise.

'You know who I'm talking about?'

'Will Fairhurst. He was Val's grandfather.'

Born in 1882, Will was the last of the seven children of William Fairhurst, a Pemberton collier, and his wife Alice Ashcroft. William senior died at the early age of forty-four when young Will was only fourteen. Alice must have struggled to bring up seven children on her own and it may be to her credit that only one of her five sons followed his father into the grindingly hard life of the pit. Like the family of Will's future bride, Mary Ann Atherton, the Fairhursts were Congregationalists in an age when an 'independent' Sunday school often involved quite a comprehensive general education in addition to religious training. Among many others, the former cabinet minister Tony Benn acknowledged the debt his own family owed to the same nonconformist tradition of mutual- and self-help. Will, like his father-in-law Peter Atherton, an ex-collier, became a Justice of the Peace.

Will and Mary Ann wanted a son but they had two daughters, Winnie and Ethel. (Reflecting on their Christian names, my mother-in-law and her sister wryly acknowledged a failure of imagination in an otherwise perfect father). Both girls also worked in the legal profession, Ethel as personal assistant to Frank Platt, a famous Wigan solicitor, and Winnie as a long-serving legal executive, specialising in inheritance and probate, with the same firm. Ethel married well-known Wigan businessman Tom Lund and they also had two daughters, my wife Val and her younger sister Margaret. A loving and even indulgent father and grandfather, all recalled that any attempt to bamboozle Will Fairhurst was doomed to abject failure. 'Those icy blue eyes could see right through me,' shuddered Ethel.

In the early years of our marriage (our children stubbornly refused to arrive until we had entered our second decade) Val and I would often drive over from Cheshire to spend the weekend in Wigan. My parents' house was small so we would usually stay with Ethel and Winnie at 12 Milton Grove in Orrell. On Friday evenings, while Ethel and Val made supper, Winnie and I would sit and chat by the fireside. I remember mentioning on one occasion that government 'initiatives' were the perennial irritations of the teaching profession.

'No sooner have we learned to do something one way than some wazzock in Whitehall tells us we now have to turn it topsy-turvy. I don't suppose you have that problem looking after your dead folks.'

'Ah, but we do. The Law is constantly changing in detail.'

'And how do you feel about that?'

'I relish it. Staying on top of the job keeps the mind supple.' This from a woman in her late seventies, who was still working in legal practice six days a week.

I remembered this conversation in sadder circumstances a few years later. Ethel, who at almost seventy looked like a trim fifty-five, had suddenly been felled by a massive stroke which left her mentally unimpaired but physically incapacitated. Visiting private nurses, procured at punishing expense, coped with the needs of the day, but Winnie, now well into her eighties, had to manage an ailing, immobile and increasingly querulous sister through the long nights. Hoping for assistance, Winnie tried to explain to Social Services that the strain of this was beyond her as she was still working full-time. 'Well, you *shouldn't* be,' was the brusque reply. There was not the slightest glimmer of recognition that a woman of eighty-odd, still at the top of her professional powers, was doing something quite remarkable which deserved support.

Val and I often think about those Friday evenings in the early years of our marriage, spent with Winnie and Ethel, the dog Oliver and the cat Lucy peacefully sharing the fireside rug. Straight-laced is an adjective which might have been invented for my mother-in-law, and anything even slightly risqué which appeared on the television screen would prompt an immediate change of channel, so we were slightly taken aback when Winnie insisted on watching a clip from the gruesome *Witchfinder General*, which some readers may remember as the film which rescued the foundering career of a notorious Hollywood over-actor. Apparently the young director Michael Reeves, unimpressed by the 'I am an established star' stuff, had made Mad Vince tone down his facial expressions to cameo proportions and the result was the performance of a lifetime. Confident that Aunty had no real interest in sex-and-sadism or the shenanigans of repressed 17th-century puritans, I thought I could identify the source of her interest. 'Do you think Vincent Price is handsome?' I asked her.

'Yes I do, rather. I love those icy blue eyes.'

I reached over to the top of the glass-fronted bookcase, picked up the framed photograph of Will Fairhurst and brought it level with the Witchfinder's image on the screen.

'Ah.'

Even in old age Winnie Fairhurst was a strikingly comely woman and in her youth she was a stunner. She never married, though of course she received a number of offers. One of them is part of family legend and connects Wigan with the American civil rights movement, not only in the volatile 1950s, but also in the present day.

The elder son of a farmer in the village of Newton-le-Willows, twenty-nine-year-old Wilson Bridge was ordained into the ministry of the Congregational church on 2 August 1935 and inducted the same day as pastor of Preston's venerable Grimshaw Street Chapel. Church elders tend to frown upon young bachelor parsons but Wilson was very willing to marry. Did he already have a young lady in his sights? Indeed he did. In fact he had two, though he probably did not share that particular piece of information with the appointing committee.

Almost exactly Wilson's age, Eleanor Sproston was the daughter of a colliery brakeman from the hamlet of Edge Green in the township of Ashton-in-Makerfield, only a cock-stride from Wilson's family home in Newton. Like his own, Eleanor's family was devoutly 'chapel'. In the reticent Lancashire phraseology of the day, Wilson and Eleanor 'liked' each other and it was clear that she would make a fine wife for a young clergyman at the beginning of his career. Wilson would not have hesitated if it had not been for Winnie Fairhurst.

As a student minister, Wilson had preached at Richmond Hill Congregational Church in Pemberton where Winnie's father Will was a founding elder. Like all visiting clergy he had been royally entertained to a splendid Sunday tea by Mary Ann and Will and their two daughters at the big rambling old house at 27 Chatsworth Street. Winnie, quite lovely and still unmarried at twenty-seven, had gently seen off several potential beaux and was happily absorbed in her legal work. Her other interest was Richmond Hill, its choir in which she sang alto, and its Sunday school, where she would patiently train the youngsters to read their poems and scriptures in clear audible voices.

Wilson, thoroughly smitten, was always received at Chatsworth Street with kindly tolerance but given no encouragement to declare his passion. In contrast, it was clear that Eleanor warmly reciprocated his interest. An agreement was reached. Wilson and Eleanor would be married by the Rev Walter D. Mason at Ashton's Gerard Street Congregational Church on 1 October 1936. All the preparations were in place, the flowers ordered, the bridesmaids briefed, the wedding dress swathed in tissue paper hanging

The icy blue eyes of Will Double–Dot Fairhurst

Winnie Fairhurst

in the wardrobe of Eleanor's family home at 311 Golborne Road, the tea-urns scoured and ready and the ladies in hats thoroughly primed for the post-nuptial bunfight.

On the very eve of his wedding, the Reverend Wilson Bridge arrived on the front doorstep of 27 Chatsworth Street in a state of dishevelment and agitation. He demanded to see Miss Fairhurst and was ushered by a somewhat alarmed Mary Ann into the parlour with its solemnly ticking grandfather clock and left to cool his heels for some long minutes while Winnie made herself presentable. When she finally arrived he did not beat about the bush. Would Winnie marry him? If she would, he would immediately go to Eleanor and tell her that their planned wedding was off. Like the Reverend St John Rivers in *Jane Eyre*, Wilson did not have to wait long for his answer. Winnie was not for him and he most definitely was not for her.

Wilson and Eleanor married as planned and Wilson proved himself to be a highly successful minister, first of all in Preston, then at Romford in Essex and at Hove, in Sussex. As a student in 1930 he had spent a month in Canada and it seems that the experience had a profound effect on him, because he and Eleanor eventually emigrated to Quebec, where Wilson had accepted the post of Pastor of the United Church of Lachute.

The 1950s was the high period of the civil rights movement in the United States of America, the era of Malcolm X and Martin Luther King. Attempts by activists to desegregate theatres, restaurants and whites-only educational institutions were being met with violence. On 4 September 1957 in Charlotte, North Carolina, a thousand miles to the south of Lachute, robed and hooded Ku Klux Klansmen picketed a theatre where a movie starring Harry Belafonte was showing, while fifteen-year-old Dorothy Counts, daughter of a black theology professor, walked with calm dignity to her enrolment at Harding High School through a spitting, jeering, missile-hurling crowd of whites. Meanwhile, racist rabble-rouser John Kasper delivered an inflammatory speech on the steps of the Mecklenburg County Courthouse calling on the white citizens of Charlotte to rise up against the school board.

'We want a heart attack, we want nervous breakdowns, we want suicides,' Kasper raved. Aware that Charlotte-born evangelist Billy Graham was scheduled to arrive from New York City the next day to support the civil rights cause, he rasped: 'Graham left here a white man but he's coming back a niggah lover.'

A hundred years previously, before the American Civil War, Canada had provided a safe haven for negroes escaping from the southern

The Rev Wilson Bridge

United States on the 'underground railroad', and it was in the dangerous atmosphere of 1957, exactly at the point when Dorothy Counts was entering Harding High School, that a white and a black pastor joined hands in an experiment in racial reconciliation which touched the lives of Christians from the Carolinas to Quebec. In August 1957, Dr E.

Raphael Michael, Pastor of the Little Rock African Methodist Episcopal Zion Church, and the Reverend Wilson Bridge of the United Church of Lachute, Quebec, exchanged pulpits, the white Reverend Bridge taking the helm of Little Rock while the black Dr Michael drove to Lachute to lead the flock there. The experiment was the idea of the Reverend Bridge and it seemed a bold step at a period when such exchanges were unknown. 'Before I left Canada friends asked me if I didn't think I was taking a risk. I laughed and replied "All of life's a risk".'

Even in the highly volatile atmosphere of 1957, a few white people braved the disapproval of the majority and joined Little Rock's black congregation to hear the Reverend Bridge, while up in Lachute Dr Michael was greeted by packed pews. He told the *Charleston News and Courier*: 'I have been an ordained minister for twenty-five years and I can safely say that in that time I have not gone into any church where I have been more welcome.'

Winnie saw Wilson only once more. It was in 1960 when he and Eleanor visited family in Lancashire with their son Alexander (rather a dish and he knew it, as my sister-in-law recalls). By this time Winnie and her widowed mother Mary Ann were living with Ethel and her husband Tom Lund at Milton Grove, and Val my future wife and her sister Margaret were in their middle teens. It was the girls who later ferreted out from Ethel and the reticent Winnie the story of the eleventh hour proposal and the romance that, Winnie continued to insist, had never been.

Winnie kept Wilson's photograph until her death at the age of ninety-three. It depicts not the ardent young suitor but a sleek, handsome, urbane and perhaps rather self-satisfied clergyman in early middle-age. I wonder if he sent it to her to show her what she had missed. I'll guess that he was a powerful and histrionic preacher (even the remark about all life being a risk is just a little bit stagy) and I am not surprised to find that he was capable of rising to the occasion at a time that needed grand gestures.

These days Charlotte prides itself on its civil rights record, but it is clear that the struggle is far from over in the South as a whole and that the Little Rock African Methodist Episcopal Zion Church is still a centre of affirmative action. As recently as 2007, three black students who sat under a 'whites-only' tree on the campus of Jena High School in Louisiana were greeted the following day by three hangman's nooses dangling from the same tree, an incident which sparked the kind of violence which has been a sporadic feature of the South throughout the past 150 years. It was the Reverend Dwayne Walker of the Little Rock Church in Charlotte who organised the protest which ensured that the pranksters got their just desserts. Allen Bethea, a colleague of the Reverend Walker, wrote: 'In 1957 the Reverends Wilson Bridge and Dr Michael each drove over 1,000 miles each way with their families in the name Christian fellowship. More than ever in this time when racial, gender, ageist, and political discord are escalating it is urgent that men and women of faith make serious and bold efforts to bridge gaps, ease tensions, erase mistrust and manifest the love of God.'

Winnie stayed with the Wigan legal firm of Frank Platt and Fishwick well into her eighties. She would never say how old she was and nobody dared ask. When she retired after sixty-four years, a staff of over fifty colleagues gathered to wish her Godspeed. It might all have been very different.

Bletchley Girls

My friend Gabriel Gorman was puzzled by the fact that whenever he let in the clutch of his Datsun, all the dashboard lights came on. 'It's quite simple,' I told him, 'this vehicle is the Irish export model. The flashing lights mean "You are now in motion".'

In 1973, 'PC' just meant 'cop'. Nobody in those days bothered much about Irish jokes, especially most of the Irish, and computers were those huge boxes you see in early *Doctor Who* re-runs or in grainy black and white photos of wartime Bletchley Park, where, incidentally (and I'll return to this in a few minutes), my friend Avril Fishwick worked as assistant to the brilliant young code-cracker Professor Asa Briggs.

These days the joke seems to be on me, because my new little portable 'netbook', vastly more powerful than the huge Bletchley 'bombes' with their bristling banks of glowing valves (relays to any Yanks out there), has taken to sending me silly messages like the ones Gabriel was getting from the Datsun. I remove my external hard drive and it tells me chattily:

'You have just unplugged a device.'

'How do you know?' I rasp. 'It might have been done by the cat.'

'You haven't even got a cat. You're allergic to cats.'

Actually, I made the last bit up. If it *could* respond in that way, I might start to believe in the 'intelligence' part of 'artificial intelligence'. But my netbook never really shows much nous, apart, that is, from a certain low cunning in finding new ways to irritate me.

I cheerfully admit to being generally incompetent in IT matters. But what a friend I have in Jesús! He runs the local informática business and he's pulled me out of many a cyber-scrape, without ever resorting to the lofty arrogance of the British 'expert' I used to patronise, or rather who used to pocket my money for the privilege of patronising me. I've just taken my old laptop in for repair and Jesús tells me with some concern: 'This one's getting a bit long in the tooth. When did you buy it?'

'About ten years ago. It's all metal and weighs almost as much as a sack of spuds, but that's not a problem because I never travel with it.

Essentially I use it as a desktop because I like the big screen.'

'It runs on the Windows XP platform.'

'I'm afraid so.'

Now, if you use a computer you probably know that real IT geeks have the same motto as detergent manufacturers: NEW! NEW! NEW! And every five minutes or so the ant-like minions infesting Silicon Valley come up with even more convoluted software to entrap the unwary. Occasionally they stumble on a real belter such as Windows XP, which is so intuitive that even I can manage it. But inevitably, whenever they've manage to produce such a cybernetic Rolls Royce, the next one will be an absolute Trabant, like Windows Vista. Even Windows Seven, which I'm running on the netbook, is better than that, though it's about as user-friendly as Val's sewing bag, i.e. vast, tangled and liable to transfix the fingers with hidden needles whenever one tries to find something which was definitely there yesterday and should be there today if one could only locate it.

If you use a computer you will know that the organisation which supplied your operating system regularly updates your software, which, among other arcane rituals, involves the PC turning itself off and re-starting. This usually happens when you are in the middle of some complicated operation such as paying a bill or submitting a tax return, which is probably why I am now tax resident in four places (the UK and Spain once each, and the USA twice) and it may even account for the bicycle to which my Barclaycard decided to treat itself some time ago, presumably for its own recreation, since I gave up biking many years back when the knees gave out.

Alas, a couple of years ago Microsoft understandably decided that after twelve years of maintaining Windows XP it had finally had enough, so Mr Gates wrote to me (personally, you understand) to inform me of that decision. First he told me rather nastily that without his support my computer would only limp along for a very short while before falling victim to one of the nastier poxes brewed up by the demon-nerds in Cyber Hades.

'But don't you fret, John,' he added chummily, 'we know you're a luser (that's geekspeak for lame user) but you'll love our new Windows B&W (Bells & Whistles). It's chock-full of NEW features and it's both

A 21st Century Bletchley Girl: Elizabeth McCaffry Payne   *Frazer Payne*

exciting (I hate that word) and challenging (but not nearly as much as I loathe that one). The only snag, from your point of view, not ours, of course, is that your antediluvian PC won't work on it. Still, if you've been running XP for the last dozen years it's more than high time you threw

137

the old junk box in the trash and bought one of our newest all-rock-singing-all dancing-on-ice models.'

With all this in mind it is refreshing to turn to a computer which is all of sixty years older than mine. Bletchley Park was essentially a six-thousand-strong band of very bright young amateurs. Avril was recruited from her Law course at Liverpool University. Some came straight from the sixth form. One girl joined at fourteen because her elder sister had been recruited, and with no parents at home there would have been nobody to look after her. She started out by making the tea and gradually slid into administration. The young amateurs were led by a few very bright, slightly older amateurs and they achieved wonders throughout World War Two, not least by beating the vastly complex Enigma coding machine used by the German military. This was remarkable enough in itself for amateurs, though even more remarkable is the fact that the only security leaks from Bletchley were deliberate ones designed to mislead the enemy. After the war, Winston Churchill, concerned about the potential Soviet threat, ordered all the Bletchley machines to be destroyed. The concern and the decision were understandable, but they put cyberscience back at least ten years, on our side of the Iron Curtain as well as on theirs.

At the time of writing Avril (89) is retired from a long career as a lawyer, a High Sheriff and a successful tilter at many windmills. Lizzie, the daughter of our dear friends Tony and Nina McCaffry, is the exact contemporary of my son Richard, and they have known each other literally from birth. As Avril did more than sixty years ago, Lizzie now works at Bletchley Park, which is a living museum. It's interesting, of course, for visitors to walk around the grounds and peer into the huts from which the likes of Asa Briggs and Alan Turing baffled the Nazis, but the latest generation of Bletchley boffins have gone one better, and if you tell young Lizzie I sent you she'll be delighted to introduce you to a working replica of one of the machines that broke Enigma.

CHAPTER 11

THE PEDANT AND THE PIRATE

Ere I go into court I will read my brief through
Said I to myself, said I
And I'll never take work I'm unable to do
Said I to myself, said I.
(From *Iolanthe* by Gilbert & Sullivan)

'You appear to be nice young people. Come to supper.'

It was a late Friday afternoon in 1968. We had just parked our elderly car in the Rectory's rhododendron-lined carriage drive and were gathering up our shopping when a lower casement window suddenly opened and two luminous, dark eyes in a long, narrow, intelligent face twinkled down at us over gold-rimmed spectacles. The tone was tenor, dry, precise, curious and, above all, friendly.

During the first year of our marriage, Val and I occupied the first-floor flat of the old All Saints' Mission House, a former Anglican nunnery in New Market Street. By the late 1960s the nuns were long gone, though our bathroom door still bore the legend 'Sister Bridget' in gold Gothic script. Just across the road was the faded Victorian splendour of Wigan Hall, the home of the Rector. The Hall, with its gatehouse, its acres of unkempt garden and its umpteen bedrooms, was a survivor of the era when comfortably beneficed clergymen kept armies of servants to look after large clerical families, but these days Canon and Mrs Park found it uncomfortably vast for themselves and their grown-up daughter, and one wing was occupied by solicitor John Hopwood Sayer and his wife Mabel. Mr Sayer, then aged eighty, was Britain's oldest serving coroner, disdainfully eschewing tape recorders and shorthand writers and taking his own notes at a stately pace with a gold-nibbed fountain pen refilled at intervals by his faithful assistant Mr Millington. In his black jacket, wing collar and pinstripes, Hoppy, as everybody called him, was a favourite Wigan character. I always think of him as the Lord

Chancellor from *Iolanthe* and a wing-collared sepia photograph of him as a young man a hundred years ago looks benevolently down at me from the wall of my little Andalucían study as I write this. And it was Hoppy himself who, without knowing us from Adam and Eve, issued that cordial invitation to supper.

As we sipped dry sherry in the Sayers' living room, we gazed with interest at what Mr Sayer called his 'rogues' gallery', a wall covered with photographs of solicitors, barristers and even, I think, a bewigged judge or two. I ventured tentatively that some members of Val's mother's family were also involved in the Law. The bright gold-spectacled gaze surveyed my twenty-three-year-old wife with renewed interest. A brief mental calculation, then 'Who was your GRANDfather?'

'Will Fairhurst.'

'Oh my word! Will and I were in chambers together when I first began practising the Law in 1907. And when we had little business in hand we often used to converse.'

Mrs Sayer smiled mischievously. 'Those conversations must have been quite frequent. In Jack's first year of practice he made exactly six shillings and eightpence in fees.'

Not at all abashed, Mr Sayer ignored the interruption and continued, 'Now I think of it, I visited your grandfather's chambers only the other day. I told the very young girl on the reception desk that I wished to see the senior partner. Much to my surprise she replied, "Yes, sir, name please?" I replied, "My name is Sayer, whom not to know argues yourself unknown."'

Mr Sayer twinkled hopefully in my direction. 'Milton,' he prompted.

'Yes, Satan challenging the guardian angels Ithuriel and Zephon in book four of *Paradise Lost*.'

'Oh my word!'

Familiar as he undoubtedly was with the ancient notion of the twin Pillars of Hercules, there is little doubt that Mr Sayer saw himself as the rock of Wigan's legal establishment. And if Hoppy were the Gibraltar, J. Basil Horsman, the clerk to the Wigan magistrates, was certainly the Jebel Musa. Softly-spoken, toothbrush-moustached and enormously tall, though with no hint of sea-green in his robust complexion, Basil discharged his duties with the incorruptibility of a latter-day Maximilien

All Saints' dignitaries preparing to set out on their Whit Walk. Jack Hopwood Sayer is the centre one of the three top-hatted figures.

Robespierre, a fact of which I have first-hand evidence. Having received my first ever 'ticket' for parking in a badly-signed no-waiting area on Dorning Street, I wrote to the bench what I thought was a fairly convincing letter of exculpation and waited on developments.

'Oh, you'll be fine,' said John Benn, who regularly covered the Magistrates' Court proceedings for the *Wigan Observer*. 'You and Basil both sing madrigals and he's a stalwart of the Music Festival committee along with your mate George Merriman. He'll put in a good word for you, you'll see.'

John told me later, 'Well, I was dead wrong. The beaks were almost taken in by your disgracefully grovelling prose, but old Basil just stared them down from somewhere up there near the ceiling and shook his head reproachfully. Result: fined five quid.'

Aloof serenity was Basil's style so, many years later at a post-Music Festival party, I was slightly taken aback at his reaction when I mentioned that Val's mother Ethel and her Aunt Winnie had both worked for solicitor Frank Platt, Wigan's Rumpole of the Bailey.

'I gather Mr Platt was rather a colourful character.'

'Colourful!' exclaimed Basil. 'Frank Platt was a pirate!'

Born in 1887, the son of a Hindley mining contractor, Frank Platt was something of an outsider as far as the Wigan legal establishment was concerned. When he set up his brass plate in 1914, solicitors were remote beings retained by wealthy clients such as mine owners and the landed gentry. Frank, a self-proclaimed radical who acted as agent for Alan Parkinson, Wigan's first Labour MP, made a point of being accessible to the kind of client who would not normally have thought of approaching a lawyer. If clients could pay, they paid. If they couldn't pay, they received the same service as those who could. Aware that visiting a solicitor's chambers could be a daunting prospect for humble folk, 'th' young turney' received many of them after office hours in his own home, and one of his children's abiding memories was the row of clients sitting self-consciously on an antique oak settle in the hallway, awaiting their turn.

In 1929, when twenty-one-year-old Winnie Fairhurst went to work as a general factotum for Frank Platt in his tank-sized office in King Street's Victoria Buildings, there was just one antiquated typewriter and an old wooden filing cabinet. Correspondence was typed with a carbon and copied with a damp cloth on a huge iron press, a tedious procedure especially if there were many letters in the day's post. Before land registration became compulsory, conveyances were written by hand. This involved going through all the deeds attached to the property, usually handwritten on vellum, a fine parchment made of animal skins which needed a dusting powder before you could write on it. (After land registration came in, many of those lovely old deeds were reincarnated as lampshades).

Life in the north of England in the 1930s was hard for struggling young solicitors, and even harder for some of their clients. Part of the insolvency procedure involved paying ten pounds into the County Court, and this became so much part of Winnie's regular duties that she became known as Wigan's Bankruptcy Queen. Her sympathy and understanding were notable both then and later, when she took over responsibility for inheritance and probate within the firm. Frank Platt's daughter Avril recalled: 'My father was always supported by Winnie. In fact he could not have managed without her. Family holidays were put on hold for fifteen minutes each day while he telephoned her.'

The firm grew, newcomers being ritually despatched to the Wallgate post office to buy 'verbal agreement stamps' (the people at the GPO were in on the joke). Ethel stayed for a few years before she married Tom Lund and became the mother of my wife Val and her sister Margaret. Avril spent World War Two at Bletchley Park as assistant to distinguished code-breakers such as Professor Asa Briggs before returning to Wigan to join her father's practice. When she married a young solicitor who was still in his RAF blue, another name was added to the growing firm, which now threatened to burst out of the cramped confines of its office space. Tom Fishwick remembered: 'When I arrived, I found Avril writing letters leaning her book against the wall because there was simply nowhere to sit.'

'Why did Basil Horsman call your old boss a pirate?' I asked Winnie and Ethel.

'In those early days,' said Winnie, 'Mr Platt did a lot of work in the courts and thanks to a primitive kind of legal-aid system he was able to represent very poor people and often he didn't charge them a penny. This, of course, was highly unpopular with the other firms.'

'And he *did* cut some corners,' added Ethel.

'In what way?'

'Well, he carried an impressive leather briefcase into court but it didn't contain any briefs.'

'I presume we're talking about legal notes and not the other things.'

'Yes of course we are, bad boy.'

'What was in Mr Platt's case, then?'

'Oh, bits and pieces, his sandwiches, his best set of teeth wrapped in a clean handkerchief, things like that.'

'So how could he do his stuff in court?'

'I was the one who carried the documents and I was expected to know them inside out. In the train on the way to a court appearance in Liverpool, for instance, the boss would say "Now then Ethel, what's this one all about?" I would give him a summary of the case and he would take it from there. Mr Platt was a brilliant actor, one of the founder members of the amateur group which eventually became Wigan Little Theatre. Any information he hadn't got he could improvise. I've seen him reduce the public gallery to tears with an impassioned plea to the Court to return a defendant to the bosom of his distraught wife and children rather than giving him a jail sentence. And all the time I knew that the chap wasn't even married.'

'I begin to understand Basil's piracy jibe.'

Frank Platt's pedantic bête noir was our old friend J. D. Hopwood Sayer and they spent many years sparring with each other, 'professional friends only', as Avril puts it. Hoppy in his prime was everyone's idea of a coroner: tall, thin and very solemn, always in black with a forbidding manner, a stickler for correct English grammar with a deadpan sense of humour which did not always come off. At an inquest on some unfortunate chap who had drowned in the canal, the police officer, referring to his notebook, read out:

'I noticed a grey gent's cap in the water.'

'Surely, officer, you really mean "a gent's grey cap"?'

'I don't know about that but the gent himself was quite grey when I got him out.'

On another occasion in the Borough Court, two men were charged with stealing a huge piece of plate glass. Just before the hearing began, a junior reporter from the *Wigan Observer*, late for court, rushed in and accidentally caught the glass so that it fell over and shattered. Hoppy, defending, immediately rose to say, 'Well, that satisfactorily removes the central piece of evidence.' But Frank Platt, prosecuting, countered, 'On the contrary, it merely increases the number of exhibits.'

Hoppy's pedantic style may have dominated in court but it cut no ice at home, where, as Val and I saw that evening in 1968, his softly spoken wife could effortlessly cut him down to size. Avril Fishwick recalls an occasion when the Sayers had invited her and several other young lawyers to dinner:

'Hoppy had discovered a new word and in his usual way was working it to death. This time it was "supernumerary" and it came into almost every sentence. Mrs Sayer, such a lovely, quiet soul, became irritated. She went into the kitchen, returned with the potatoes still in their roasting tin which she rattled down on the table in front of her husband. Hoppy was horrified.'

'Mab! Where are the vegetable dishes?'

'I decided that they were *supernumerary*.'

The Spy Who Went Out Into The Cold

'Hello, boys, I'm Margery Booth from Wigan!'

The young Lancashire lass's breezy greeting to the British prisoners may have amused their German guards, but they were probably more than a bit disturbed when she insisted on ending all her concerts with 'Land of Hope and Glory'. No doubt she got away with it because, in this strangest of all POW camps, most of the staff were Anglophiles. The fact that she was on first name terms with Adolf Hitler may also have helped.

Born in Hodges Street, Wigan, in 1906, to Levi Booth and his wife Florence, the teenage Margery could hardly have dreamed where her fine singing voice would take her when she first began lessons with a Bolton teacher, though she rapidly graduated to London's Guildhall School of Music, winning the Mercers' and Opera scholarships and the prestigious Liza Lehmann Prize. On 4 October 1935 she made her debut at the Queen's Hall, not the posh one in London, but the Methodist mission in Market Street which has launched the career of many a Wigan singer. Those old Victorian 'methodies' knew a thing or three about acoustics, and though the hall could accommodate 2,500 people, its galleried horseshoe shape carried every note from the platform with crystal-clear focus to the most distant seat in the house.

A year later, Margery Booth sang at Covent Garden as Maddelena in Verdi's

Margery Booth

Rigoletto, and she went on to sing the title role in *Carmen* and then Amneris in a Hollywood movie of *Aida*, before her marriage to Dr Egon Strohm, son of a wealthy Black Forest brewing family, permanently shifted the focus of her career to Germany. There, an appearance in Wagner's *Parsifal* at Bayreuth brought her to the attention of Hitler, who swept into her dressing room and presented her with two hundred red roses wrapped in a swastika-printed sash with a card signed 'Adolf'. Undoubtedly the Führer and his propaganda minister Josef Goebbels, both genuine opera buffs, appreciated the beautiful voice, but their adulation also had an ulterior motive.

Stalag IIID at Genshagen was known as 'the Holiday Camp'. It had been set up by Dr Goebbels and broadcaster William Joyce, notorious in Britain as Lord Haw Haw, to persuade Allied prisoners to join the new British Free Corps and fight against Britain's ally Soviet Russia. They had already managed to recruit John Amery, son of a member of Churchill's War Cabinet (sixty-five years later, his character became the basis for an episode of the TV series *Foyle's War*) and they hoped that, gently treated, more prisoners would follow suit. Margery Booth, married to a German and confidently thought to be a Nazi sympathiser, was to be part of the treatment. With a ready smile and a voice like an angel, she was also very easy on the eye, as photographs taken in the camp vividly show.

Marjorie's Genshagen concerts took on a darker dimension when John Brown arrived in the camp in 1943. Far from being a POW and a potential defector, parts he played with total conviction, Brown was an utterly ruthless British agent working for MI9, the intelligence branch implacably dedicated to ferreting out and eliminating traitors. Rapidly winning the confidence of Amery and his Nazi masters, Brown used Margery as a courier for messages to his London controller, and on one famous occasion she is reputed to have sung before Hitler with secret documents hurriedly secreted in her scanties.

Margery had been given assurances by Hitler and Goebbels that they would deal personally with any insult she received because of her British birth, but the indemnity naturally did not cover espionage, and when Brown's activities were discovered by the Nazis, she was arrested and repeatedly interrogated by the Gestapo. Any admission would have ended in a grisly death for her and her contacts, but Margery did not crack and was eventually released for lack of evidence. Escaping from Berlin during the chaos of an RAF bombing raid, she fled to Bavaria, where she was picked up by the advancing Americans. Her intrepid spymaster John Brown had already made his own exit by killing a German colonel and stealing his staff car.

After the war, information provided by Brown and Margery was used at the Old Bailey to convict Joyce and Amery, both of whom were hanged for treason though many were disturbed by the execution of Joyce, who was an Irish subject. As for John Amery, who calmly pleaded guilty and declined to offer any defence, the executioner Albert Pierrepoint later wrote that he had never hanged a braver man.

Ironically, it was among the austerities of victorious post-war Britain that Margery Booth discovered that she had played her final role too well. Vilified as a collaborator, her singing career was in ruins. When she emigrated to New York in 1951 she was already desperately ill with the cancer which eventually killed her at the age of only forty-seven. So far, her courage in risking her life for her country has been unrecognised and calls for a posthumous George Cross have gone unheeded.

Currently there is talk of a film of her exploits in Nazi Germany, so perhaps at last the girl from Hodges Street with the lovely voice is about to receive the recognition she deserves.

CHAPTER 12

EVA THE DIVA

Question: How many divas does it take to change a light bulb?
Answer: One. She holds the bulb and the world revolves around her.

'Aunty.'

'Yes, dear?'

'Is that a hermaphrodite?'

'No, dear, a mezzo-soprano.'

Was that sublime innocence real or assumed? Part of Dame Eva's charm was her ability to keep us all guessing, and this smart alec ten-year-old great-nephew, sitting with her in her box at Covent Garden, could never be sure as to just whose leg was being pulled. With some folk you can be reasonably sure that what you see is what you get, but divas are different. And let me be clear from the outset that when I write 'diva', I don't just mean somebody more or less female who can manage to squawk through a tune with the help of an amplifier the size of Birmingham and a plethora of technology to disguise the worst of the bum notes.

A couple of nights ago I suffered through the first part of the Eurovision Song Contest, that blatant triumph of packaging over content. The contest, of course, has been a joke for decades, but the standard of this one was so abysmal that the appearance of Fathers Ted and Dougal with 'My Lovely Horse' would have been a vastly greater relief than Poland's mammary masturbatory fantasy. But the really mad thing was the telly gurus the following day, claiming that the contest being won by a bloke in a bad false beard and a frock was a triumph for a new and original kind of diva. A bearded lady! Original? For God's sake, have these people never been to a fairground?

Diva means 'goddess' in Italian. The original divas were the great stars of the operatic stage and all of them were sopranos. Pundits have been predicting the demise of bel canto, the art of beautiful singing, for the past seventy years or more, but there's an old theatrical adage to the effect that the critics are like the eunuchs in the harem. They can all tell you exactly how it should be done. They see it done every night, but when it comes to doing it themselves... So the claim that the golden age of opera ended with the start of the Second World War is as daft as a CD title I read the other day mourning the fat man from Modena as 'Pavarotti, the Last Tenor'. In fact, the diva's anthem (another sadly debased word) ought to be 'I Have Survived'. Renée Fleming is a diva. So is Ana María Martinez. So are Angela Gheorghiu and Anna Netrebko. And forget the large lady in the horned helmet, because in addition to astounding voices and immaculate techniques, these girls all have film star looks.

Attractive opera singers, though arguably more common now than in the past, are nothing new. English sopranos of the early 20th century, when Eva Turner made her debut, were often pretty, but the operatic world in general expected them to sound under-powered and genteel. In those days, foreign opera houses never thought of engaging an English singer and the English houses themselves imported troops of foreigners. The young Eva, with her generous curves and cloud of curly blonde hair, was certainly easy on the eye, but the sound she made was far from genteel or small. She was a little lass, which made the sheer size and glittering brilliance of that voice all the more amazing. Recordings give some idea of it, but the living reality must have been astounding. Covent Garden's Artistic Director claimed that her top C projected straight through the back wall of the Royal Opera House and out into Bow Street. When Eva recorded operatic ensembles, the engineers had to place her well behind the other soloists, the chorus and the orchestra to achieve any kind of balance. And when she became a great lady with a villa on the Swiss side of Lake Lugano, folk living on the opposite Italian shore would open their windows to listen to her practising and then telephone for an encore. But don't run away with the idea that she always sang loudly. Listen to her recording of 'Ritorna Vincitor', where she spins the most delicate pianissimo thread through Aida's prayer without losing a jot of that silvery tone.

Eva Turner was born at 5, Goddard Street, Werneth, Oldham on 10 March 1892, but her roots were sunk deep in the Wigan area. Her father Charles, who worked as an engineer at Manor Mill, had been born in 1866 in Standish, where the Turner family had been settled since Charles's grandfather Daniel, a weaver from Wrightington, married an Almond Brook girl called Margaret Morris at St Wilfrid's Church on 13 August 1827. From the age of seven, Eva not only knew she had a voice but also what she wanted to do with it, and actress Marie, wife of the tenor Tom Burke, recalled her wistful 'Ee, Mrs Burke, do you think I'll ever be an opera singer?'

Eva's dreamy artistic mother and her practical down-to-earth father were happy to underwrite her talent. Her first formal singing lessons were with Dan Rootham, the teacher of the famous contralto Dame Clara Butt, and from 1911 to 1914 she studied at the Royal Academy of Music. Too many young singers have ruined their voices by taking on too much too early in their careers but on the threshold of the Great War, with few professional opportunities available, there was little danger of that, and Eva began her career as a humble member of the chorus of the Carl Rosa touring company at a salary of £2 a week. Soon she began to take on bit parts and then leads, with an extra ten bob in the wage packet.

A soloist in a small opera company had to be as adaptable as an actor in 'rep', and Eva recalled: 'Many times I sang four performances, heavy roles such as *Meistersinger, Tannhauser, Il Trovatore* and *Aida*, and I was in excellent voice at the end of the week, so I thought to myself "well, I must be doing something right".' She told the *Wigan Observer*: 'It was a severe life. England was under the shadow of the Great War. Travelling was arduous, food was scarce, and I always seemed to be losing my coupons. One night we were locked up from midnight till dawn at Carlisle station. Enemy aeroplanes were about, and to add to our discomfort the station was in blackout. It wasn't a pleasant experience for a cold and hungry company. Again, at York, all the lights went out and we had to finish *The Tales of Hoffman* by candlelight.'

In 1920, to public and press acclaim, Eva made her debut at the Royal Opera House, Covent Garden, as Santuzza in *Cavalleria Rusticana*, and four years later came an invitation to La Scala, to meet the great Arturo Toscanini. The Carl Rosa had performed exclusively in English, and for her Milan audition she sang Aida's aria 'Ritorna Vincitor' because it was the only piece she knew in Italian. A few months later she was conversing

Eva Turner, the Definitive Turandot

so fluently in the language that Italians meeting her for the first time found it hard to believe that she was a foreigner. Italian audiences in those days were very intolerant of foreign singers and somebody at La Scala suggested that it would be prudent for Eva to Italianise her name. Her brusque refusal had far-reaching consequences, not only for her but for the world of opera. More than forty years later, when she was in Canada to judge an opera contest, the *Montreal Times* commented: 'It is largely due to her pioneering success, and her persistent refusal to change her name, that today's singers can answer curtain calls in the greatest opera houses of the world with an English name.'

Eva Turner was the very first English artist to sing at La Scala, and the rest, as the cliché goes, is history. Great theatres all over Italy, Germany and South America clamoured to book the little lass from Oldham. She was heard in Rome, Naples, Las Palmas, Buenos Aires, Caracas and Rio de Janeiro. She became a regular of the Chicago Opera, with colleagues whose starry names bejewel the firmament of great singing. And the most distant member of an audience of twenty thousand at the Pasadena Bowl heard her as clearly as if she had been singing in his front parlour. But, an enduring sadness, the New York Metropolitan, remained aloof, and only invited her at the very end of her career when she knew that the wonderful voice had lost some of its bloom and could no longer be trusted to make the perfect statement she would have wanted.

I was about to write that, of all the roles Eva Turner sang in a thirty-four-year international career, the one with which she is most associated is that of Puccini's *Turandot*. Then I paused, because that statement is utterly inadequate. Eva Turner simply *was* Turandot. Dare I breathe it, she *is* Turandot because no soprano has ever equalled her as Puccini's terrifying princess, terrifying not only because of her disturbing habit of executing her suitors, but also because in this role, and especially in the main soprano aria, Puccini challenges the very limits of the human voice.

Turandot is set in a mythical imperial China, in a palace presided over by a beautiful young woman obsessed with a thousand-year-old tragedy. Princess Turandot's gentle ancestress Lu Ling was ravished and murdered by invading Tartars, and Turandot has vowed to avenge her upon the whole race of men. Noble suitors, who travel from the ends of the earth to seek her hand in marriage, must solve three riddles or die, and as the curtain goes up, the luckless Prince of Persia awaits the headman's axe. In the great aria 'In Questa Reggia', Turandot taunts yet another challenger, Prince Calaf, who eventually emerges as the hero of the story: 'Stranger! Do not tempt fortune! The riddles are three but death is one.' Naturally, Calaf, being a hero, a tenor, and, quite possibly a habitual solver of the *Times* crossword, has no problem puzzling out the conundrums, crying out passionately that the riddles may be three but love is one.

What is born each night and dies at dawn? Hope, obviously.

What flickers red and warm like a flame, yet is not fire? Blood (another easy one in this most sanguinary of kingdoms). The Princess is on tenterhooks. All the other candidates were reassuringly dim, and nobody else has got this far.

What is like ice, yet burns? Turandot, of course.

Calaf, who has been travelling incognito, then goes on to turn the tables on the princess by offering to release her from marrying him if she can discover his name before the next sunrise. In panic, Turandot decrees that in the search for the elusive name 'No one shall sleep tonight!', a command mockingly echoed in the aria 'Nessun Dorma', which Luciano Pavarotti turned into a World Cup hit. The slave girl Liu, who adores the Prince and hates the thought of his marrying the iceberg princess, reveals his identity, but it is too late. The utterly smitten Turandot declares, 'No, the name is not Calaf, it is Love.' So they live happily ever after. Or do they? Nobody knows for sure because Puccini died before he could finish the opera.

There are five extant recordings of Eva Turner singing 'In Questa Reggia'. The most frequently heard is the one she made in Westminster Hall in 1928. Forget modern recording studios with their multiple takings-out and splicings-in. This 'In Questa' was recorded in one 'take' with a single microphone suspended high in the roof, but in spite of these primitive conditions the sense of flight and the gleaming expansion of the upper register are exhilarating. Hearing the record for the umpteenth time a knowledgeable commentator writes: 'Those high Cs still chill me to the bone as much as the Prince of Persia facing the block.'

Eva's final performance at Covent Garden in 1948 was of course in this role which she had made so much her own a quarter of a century before. Wartime austerities were forgotten and a reviewer wrote: 'Eva Turner gives a Titanic performance as Turandot. No ordinary mortal could sustain such a role as this and at the same time manoeuvre a costume such as she wears in the first act – a blue and gold train that would nearly carpet Piccadilly Circus, borne along in her wake by a beauty chorus of six.' One of those beauties was thirteen-year-old Millicent Martin who was to make such a hit ten years later in *That Was the Week, That Was*.

You don't stop being a diva when you leave the operatic stage, though different divas have different styles in retirement. Renata Tebaldi maintained a retinue and played the grande dame right to the end, looking unnervingly like my Aunt Maud. (This, incidentally, is not to denigrate either lady. Maud, also a soprano, was a lovely woman with a strong resemblance to the young Celia Johnson, though with a vibrato approximately as wide as Ainsdale sands). Many great singers who have outlived their voices find it painful to listen to their successors, but Dame Eva was an avid opera-goer right to the end of her long life, and her ninetieth birthday was celebrated with a gala concert at Covent Garden. If you look on *YouTube* you will find a fascinating conversation between her and the young Placido Domingo, whom she had heard as Otello at the Garden the previous evening. She 'appeared' on *Desert Island Discs* no less than three times, though she so resolutely refused to choose any of her own records that for the third occasion the BBC had to insist on prefacing the half hour with an extra recording. It was of course 'In Questa Reggia'. It was in this programme that she told the story of the bouncing prima donna which has become part of operatic anecdotage. In the last act of Puccini's *Tosca* the heroine throws herself off the battlements of the Castel Sant'Angelo. The drop at Hull's Alexandra Theatre was shallow and Eva recalled: 'I threw myself down on to the trampoline with much force and came bounding up again.'

Eva Turner was fifty-seven years old when she retired from the operatic stage in 1948, and she died in 1990 aged ninety-eight. Those intervening forty-two years were long enough for a second career and even a third, and that is exactly what happened, because Eva reinvented herself twice. Her first new avatar was as a singing teacher. This may sound obvious but it isn't, because many opera stars fail as teachers because though they may sing wonderfully, they really haven't much idea of how they do it. Eva Turner wasn't just a good teacher. She was a great one. But the odd thing is that this diva of Covent Garden and La Scala began her teaching career, of all unlikely places, in a one horse town in the American Midwest. Joseph Benton, a former operatic colleague (he had sung as Giuseppe Bentonelli, which tells its own story) was now a member of the music department of Oklahoma University and, reading of Eva's retirement from the stage, suggested to the university's president that she should be invited to join the faculty. Eva agreed to go for a nine-month period and stayed for ten years. Her students came to love her, but that was only after she had made it clear how things were going to be. One bumptious young man recalled: 'I went into my audition with her, very much "Mr It". Miss Turner listened to me sing, then closed the piano, looked me straight in the eye and said "I will accept you as a student, however we are going to have an extreeemely difficult year."' She gave much shorter shrift to 'reds-under-the-bed' Senator Joseph McCarthy when he accused her of being a dangerous political radical and demanded that she sign an oath of allegiance to the USA: 'I am a British subject and will do no such thing.'

Eva returned to London in 1959, where she was appointed Professor of Singing at the Royal Academy of Music, a position she held until well into her eighties, not infrequently clashing with colleagues who knew much less about the world of opera than she did. Her pupils included such towering talents as Amy Shuard, Gwyneth Jones and Kiri Te Kanawa. Not a few found her too demanding. Most singers dislike using their voices early in the day but when a youngster complained at being given the 8 a.m. slot Eva merely struck a chord on the piano and sang, from 'cold', the final passage from 'In Questa Reggia', with its three consecutive high Cs. 'That's how I made my name, dear. How will you make yours?' After retiring from the Royal Academy she continued to teach at a fraction of the going rate. It wasn't that she was uninterested in money (forty years before it became fashionable she recycled everything from wire coat-hangers to plastic bags) but she was infinitely more interested in nurturing talent.

Eva Turner was created a Dame of the British Empire in 1960 and that was the point at which she embarked on her third career. Operatic diva, distinguished teacher and now media star. I first became aware of her as a popular chat show guest in the 1970s when she was already over eighty. Look again at that conversation with Domingo and marvel at the sheer energy of this little woman, well into her ninth decade, and imagine her at thirty or forty. Enthusiastic, ebullient, even slightly dotty, with her sweeping gestures, over-enunciated speech and extravagantly rolled 'r's, she might have stepped straight out of the cast of the then popular *Hinge and Bracket* TV show, in which two countertenors in drag poked gentle fun at the operatic mannerisms of yesteryear. In fact, she was as great a fan of theirs as Margaret Thatcher was of *Anyone for Dennis?* and Dame Hilda and Dr Evadne appeared in her ninetieth birthday gala along with the greatest opera and theatre stars of the day, including her former pupil Patricia Routledge, who really could sing when she wasn't terrorising the neighbours as Hyacinth Bucket.

Eva never lost touch with her roots. Another Dame, Gracie Fields, was a great friend and the operatic Dame would imperceptibly lapse back into 'Lanky' when the two of them were together. Her father Charles had retired to Ashton-in-Makerfield and on various occasions Eva sang both there and at the Hippodrome in Wigan. Charles continued to attend all her 'home' performances and in 1935 he died quietly from heart failure while waiting in the audience at Covent Garden to hear his daughter sing in Weber's *Der Freischutz*. He and his wife Elizabeth are buried in the family grave at St Wilfrid's in Standish, where Eva Turner, the greatest diva of them all, joined them in 1990 at the great age of ninety-eight.

Who Do I Know You're Not?

Leanne and I are both descended from Catharine Edwards, born in 1780 at Llanidan on the Isle of Anglesey in a house intriguingly named Wrach Ddu (The Black Witch). Leanne lives in Michigan and I live in Andalucía. Last October, in the USA, we met for the first time in the flesh (if I dare put it that way without being misoverestimated) but over the past ten years we've encountered each other numerous times in cyberspace and exchanged stacks of family documents and photos by email. We first met on a website where thousands of us genealogy fanatics keep our family trees. One of the features of the site is that a member can see if another member's tree overlaps with his own. Enter Sheila, messaging me from Melbourne: 'Isn't this bonza? We're fifth cousins umpteen times removed!'

Not everybody is so fired with family history. Take my wife, for instance. (No! I'll resist that old chestnut because I love her dearly and for a small woman she does pack a surprisingly effective right hook). I sometimes get up as early as five o'clock to mine a promising genealogical seam and by the time I take Val her morning coffee, at about seven, I often have a fresh chunk of ore to share.

'What do you think a puddler was?'

'Something to do with iron?'

'Yes!' It seems that my great-aunt Polly's first husband George's father Bill was a puddler. In the Black Country, would you believe? They lived at Oldbury in Staffordshire at number seven Pig Lane. I bet that address hasn't survived into the twenty-first century.'

'John...'

'Yes, darling?'

'Bugger off.'

'Not very parliamentary language. What would your mother think of that?'

'She'd know exactly where I got it from. Now go away and let me drink my coffee in peace.'

Loving spouses are supposed to tolerate one's foibles for better or for worse, but the *Ancient Mariner* approach – he holds him with his glittering eye – is generally frowned upon at dinner parties, so I always hesitate before revealing to a new acquaintance that I am President of the Wigan Klavern of the All-Too-Audible Empire of Genealogy Bores. But a surprising number of people do find family history anything but tedious, and one of the standard questions (particularly appropriate in the year when the humble grave of Richard III was discovered) is 'Have you dug up any skeletons?' In both my wife's case and mine the answer is 'yes', and some of the bodies lie a lot closer to home than King Richard's Leicester car park. I remember the audience's shocked laughter forty years ago when a contestant on a TV quiz show introduced himself as Fred Bastard.

'Isn't that a rather unusual name?' queried the quiz master.

'Not where I live,' was the stolid reply, 'there's hundreds of us Bastards down in Devon.'

Well, there were quite a few in Victorian Lancashire, and if I had a family escutcheon it would probably include more bends sinister than the Anglezarke Pass. This takes me rather neatly to the other standard question: 'Are you descended from anybody "important"?' In my case the answer appears to be a definite 'not really'. I can muster at least fifteen generations of farmers, a company of coalminers, a body of brass-finishers, several publicans, the odd draper and a stroppy excise officer turned schoolmaster, but I'm fairly sure I don't share Shakespeare's DNA. Thanks to an amazingly clever website, which includes my great-great-grandfather, born in 1802, I can trace one of my lines of descent to the 12th-century Corfields of Corfhull, a Shropshire village which disappeared at the time of the Black Death of 1349. My grandmother's family, the Sharrocks, were minor Lancashire gentry in the same period and though my cousin Brian says we are actually Chiracs who came over with the Conqueror I have so far found no evidence to support that claim. Val, incidentally, is descended from Michael Jackson. No, not that one. Her M. J. was an 18th-century doctor in Upholland, and though he might not have been much of a singer he probably did have a viable nose.

The desire to be a 'somebody' rather than a 'nobody' does seem to be deeply rooted. Louise lives in Tasmania and we are both descended

Matthew Boulton and his Manufactory   *Andy Lidstone/ Bigstock*

from Lizzie Lowe, born in Haigh, in 1846. My grandmother Annie was Lizzie's legitimate daughter. Louise's grandfather George was Lizzie's mistake, born before her happy marriage to my great-grandfather James Sharrock. Now, as it happens, all of our ancestors worked on the estate of the Earl of Crawford and Balcarres, so Louise tells me 'George was fathered by Lord Crawford and of course, like all young aristocrats, he was privately educated.' Complete tosh of course. George was fathered by A. N. Other (who had such a busy time throughout the 19th century that he must certainly have had a bike) and went to the village school where they did such a good job of educating him that he found a responsible position at the technological cutting edge, delivering telegrams, the email messages of the late Victorian era.

So I'm not a 'somebody', but thanks to my son Richard's marriage to Minnesota-born Christine, two of my grandchildren really are related to characters who have fretted and strutted their brief hour upon the stage of history. In addition to Daniel the Regicide, whom we met in Chapter 7, they include among their other relations: Elihu Yale, endower of the great Ivy League university; Owain Glyndwr, that highly successful rebel against King Henry IV; and, believe it or not, Winston Churchill. How do I know all this? The answer is that in tracing their ancestry back a mere 200 years via the US national and state censuses, I came across the all-important 'gateway ancestor', which links Joseph and Claire's line to gentry whose pedigree has been reliably 'done' by professional genealogists.

Libraries and local archives are helpful, of course, but there is such a plethora of material online that one has to be very scrupulous about sifting it. Errors abound on the Internet and some folk who are new to genealogy (and some who are not so new and should know better) are seduced by wishful thinking into daft conclusions. Re-enter Sheila, my Melbourne 'cousin'.

'We are both descended from Ellen Healey, born in Wigan in 1832,' she gushes. 'I've traced Ellen's emigration to Australia in 1880. She met my great-great-grandfather Bruce in Melbourne and I'm descended from their third daughter Edna. Have a look at my tree.'

I had a look. So Bruce, aged twenty-one, was bowled over by Ellen, aged forty-eight, and they proceeded to marry and have seven kids? I think not. Especially as I know for a fact that Ellen married engineer Richard Clough and died in Wigan in 1885. They were my great-great-grandparents. Incidentally, Richard Clough's grandfather, another Richard, was connected with a major 'somebody', being employed as an engineer at the Soho (Birmingham) 'manufactory' of Matthew Boulton, one of the greatest figures of the second Industrial Revolution. And Matthew Boulton's detested rival was the ruthless 'Copper King', Thomas Williams of Llanidan, Anglesey. How's that for geographical full-circularity?

CHAPTER 13

POP SKIRROW BATTERS BONAPARTE

Pop Skirrow is a grand old man.
The Romans knew him well...

The official lyric of our cringingly embarrassing school song actually began with a jocular reference to Wigan's supposed origin as Coccium, a 1st-century military way-station, but we preferred our racier version. To an outsider it might have sounded a trifle disrespectful, but any member of Wigan Grammar School, from the headmaster down to the merest first-form piglet, would have recognised it as a tribute to one of the school's best-loved and most memorable of characters.

Geoff Dykes, who joined WGS in August 1964 as head of the History Department, was an excellent teacher. He knew it and he was not shy of letting his pupils know that he knew it. By the usual schoolboy consensus almost every newly arrived member of staff was rapidly allotted a nickname and the loftily superior Dykes was immediately hailed as 'God'. And as he was habitually sparing with praise, the rare student who gained his approval was likely to find himself ironically apotheosed by his classmates as 'Jesus, my belovéd son in whom I am well pleased'.

Given that his excellent History results fully supported his pretensions to deity, Dykes no doubt found it galling that so many pupils, past and present, appeared to look back through rose-tinted spectacles on the long reign of his predecessor, whose farewell dinner had been the Old Boys' Association's best-attended event in many years. 'Ah yes, Mr Dykes, there is no doubt that the department needed dragging into the Swinging Sixties, but we all have such affectionate memories of Mr Skirrow.'

Philip Wilson Skirrow, 'Pop' to generations of us, had joined the school in 1932 and according to which version you believed had been inspiring his pupils or boring them witless ever since. I will readily admit that I was one of the inspired, and though I have been fascinated by the past for as long as I can remember, Pop's enthusiasm for his subject and, above all, his anecdotes, added a special spice to the Stuart period and the Napoleonic wars. An assiduous marker of essays (not always true of schoolmasters of that era) Pop praised my English style while regularly taking me to task for my vagueness about dates and treaties, my bias in favour of the Cavaliers (wrong but romantic) and my unreasoning prejudice against the Roundheads (right but repulsive).

'Waffle, woolly-minded, sentimental, uncritical monarchist waffle,' muttered my mate Gordon Parr, a real historian in the making, when Mr Skirrow awarded my airy flights of fancy the same marks as his scholarly interpretations of the facts.

When I joined the school in 1957, Skirrow was already about sixty years old. He didn't teach the small fry, but we were aware of him as one of the presiding pantheon which also included such august figures as Joe Boswell, Sav Savigny and Dicky Nutt. Tallish, spare, tweed-suited, with a handsome neatly rounded head and crew-cut, curly, iron-grey hair, Pop floated serenely along the parqueted corridors in an academic gown of astonishing disreputability, worn 'off the shoulder' in a travesty of an early 1950s ball gown. From time to time younger members of staff, including me when I returned to WGS as a master in 1967, would attempt to ape Pop's distinctive décolletage, but nobody else ever managed to carry off rags with such style.

In his A Level classes, Skirrow did not so much teach as lecture. He invariably arrived in the classroom with one of the two ancient and tattered manuscript books which held his English and European notes, though throughout the two years of the A Level course I never saw him refer to either of them, for like Chaucer's Pardoner he could fairly claim that 'I kan by rote al that I telle'. This might have implied that his interest in historical research had stopped short when he had received his B Litt from Oxford in about 1920, but in fact one of our main English History textbooks was Christopher Hill's *The Century of Revolution*, a recently published Marxist interpretation of the Stuart period and a surprisingly adventurous choice for an elderly History teacher in a provincial grammar school.

Though he neither smoked nor toped, Pop had the kind of voice which is often thought to be redolent of old port and Havana cigars, and I was later to make use of it when playing the role of Sir Toby Belch in *Twelfth Night*. Pop's classroom style was theatrical and there were times when we realised that he had suddenly become part of his own narration. 'Eighteen hundred and four. There were we in our Martello towers... looking out over the English Channel... (An imaginary telescope was opened and panned intently across an invisible expanse of choppy grey water) ...anxiously scanning the horizon for Napoleon's flat-bottomed boats... (The imaginary telescope, clapped decisively shut, was carefully placed on an imaginary windowsill and a mythical Brown Bess musket was hefted, levelled and noisily cocked) ...crammed to the gunwales with garlic-munching... French... Froggies.'

At these moments Pop's vocal delivery was measured and portentous and Barry Lown, a Yorkshire lad who claimed that his surname derived from the Leuwen family of William of Orange, developed the habit of providing a sotto voce counterpoint to the Skirrow rhetoric.

Pop: But was Lord Nelson intimidated by the nautical minions of the Little Corporal?
Barrie: Was he f...
Pop: Not a bit of it!

At other times, impelled by the exigencies of the syllabus, Pop raced ahead at breakneck speed. As we were never taught to take notes, I was left forever scribbling hopelessly in the rear of the discourse, and later when I attempted to revise for examinations I would fail miserably to decipher my wretched scrawl and revert to making my own summaries of Hill and Trevelyan. Writer's cramp was a permanent condition in Skirrow's classes, and we all had strategies for coping with it, including Pop himself, whose swathes of solid instruction were carefully interspersed with what he called 'stories', those curious anecdotes with which History and indeed the whole of human life is strewn: Captain Jenkins, whose pickled ear, produced in Parliament, became the pretext for a war against Spain; the cloaked and muffled midnight figure of Cromwell murmuring 'cruel necessity' over the corpse of King Charles I; the urn containing the imperfectly pickled viscera of La Grande

Mademoiselle detonating noisily during her funeral and decorating the assembled mourners with its gruesome contents.

King Louis XIV of France, whether dead or alive, was a particular favourite, and one of the quirkier anecdotes concerned that mighty monarch's heart. As we knew from the story of Louis' sister, the practice when interring the bodies of the noble deceased was to preserve the internal organs in separate containers from the embalmed corpse. Pop told us that when the Revolutionary mob broke into the royal tombs in the 1790s one of the irreverent sans-culottes pocketed the mummified heart of the Sun King, who had died in 1715. During the next century this macabre souvenir passed through several hands until it was finally produced at an antiquarian society dinner in London during the mid-Victorian period.

'And this, gentlemen, is my *pièce de résistance*: the heart of Le Roi Soleil, His Christian Majesty King Louis XIV of France.'

By this time, with age and much handling, the heart had shrivelled to the size of a walnut and it was apparent that the assembled guests were less than impressed with its provenance as a human organ. One of them, a geologist by profession, suspecting that this small, hard black object was in fact some kind of rock sample, placed it on his tongue, which is apparently the sort of thing mineralogists do when faced with such a puzzle. It was at this point that the butler, entering with the decanter of port, jogged the scientist's elbow. Result: violent choking, bulging eyes, rapid asphyxiation and death in an era long before the Heimlich manoeuvre was discovered.

'And that,' Pop concluded solemnly, 'is how the heart of King Louis XIV of France came to find its final resting place inside a deceased geologist in a Victorian English cemetery.'

Pop was an exceptionally fit for a man of his age and a distinctive Skirrow trademark was his habit of doing discreet handsprings without ever interrupting the flow of his teaching. As I scribbled furiously in an attempt to keep up with the narrative, Gordon Parr would nudge me and mutter 'He's levitating again.' We would break off our note-taking and watch with fascination as, with hands placed flat on the desktop in the nine o' clock–three o' clock position, Pop straightened his arms and lifted his neat brown brogues six inches off the floor. He could maintain this feat apparently without effort for minutes on end, certainly for much longer than any of us youngsters could, and many a junior member of staff came an ignominious cropper while trying to emulate it.

Another gleefully-imitated mannerism was Pop's habit of scratching his chin with his right arm looped over the top of his head in almost a full circle, a trick I could do in my supple teens, though it defeats me now that I am about the age Pop was then. You could always identify WGS A Level History students. They were the ones who loped around the quadrangle in three-hundred-and-sixty-degree chin-scratching mode, like demented orangutangs, cackling maniacally and muttering, 'You know, gentlemen, Louis XIV had some rather peculiar habits.'

There were never enough of Pop's anecdotes to satisfy either our appetite for stories or our thirst for distractions to enliven the long tranches of lecturing which numbed the brain and paralysed the writing hand, so we became adept at devising red herrings of various kinds. Clive Meadows, whose brand-new Lotus Europa later became a minor local press sensation by being so ridiculously low-slung that it would not operate the electronic barrier of the Millgate multi-storey car park, was already at seventeen endowed with the apparently guileless sincerity which was to make him the doyen of Wigan estate agents. When we were in the lower sixth, the Local Education Authority was well into the process of planning to amalgamate WGS with the neighbouring Thomas Linacre School. While most of us regarded this plan with equanimity, we were well aware that many of the staff, including Pop Skirrow, did not, a fact which Clive exploited with ruthless cunning.

'I'm very worried about this amalgamation, Sir.'

'Ah, Meadows, no one understands your concern better than I, but reflect, dear boy, that the school has passed through many changes and chances in the four hundred and sixty years of its existence and this is only one of them. Have I ever told you how Bonnie Prince Charlie broke all our windows?'

'No Sir! How fascinating!'

'Yes, yes, Sir! Do tell. Did he use a pistol?'

'No, no, foolish fellow, he didn't do it personally of course. He was a well-brought-up young man and I'm sure he must have regretted such vandalism, however…'

As an old hand, Pop netted most of our red herrings before they fairly had the chance to swim, but even so there were notable triumphs. The Day of the Serpent was one of them. Gown akimbo, Pop was expatiating on some such turgid theme as the Grand Remonstrance when Clive's 'concerned' tones cut across the discourse:

'Sir! Talbot has a snake on his desk!'

'Not today, thank you, Meadows.'

The class, carefully primed, joined in the chorus: 'But, Sir, a snake!'

'Nonsense. And you, Talbot, kindly remove the toy or whatever you have on your desk.'

'It's not a toy, Sir. It's a snake.'

'Rubbish.'

'A live one, Sir.'

'Poppycock.'

'Honestly, Sir!'

'Balderdash. Meadows, this feeble attempt at distraction is far below even your customarily abysmal standard.'

'I find that remark deeply hurtful, Sir.'

'I am very pleased to hear it. Now, can we get on?'

'So reptiles are actually allowed in school then, Sir?'

Pop attempted manfully to forge ahead with the Grand Remonstrance but we could see that a niggling worm of doubt had wriggled into his mind. Still lecturing he sidled towards Godfrey Talbot's desk at the back of the class, peered short-sightedly then stopped dead in silent astonishment at the sight of the three-foot grass snake draped nonchalantly around Godfrey's neck.

'God bless my soul! It really is a serpent.'

'Told you, Sir.'

'Very well. An excellent prank demonstrating more imagination than I had hitherto given any of you credit for.'

'Oh, Sir! That's—'

'—deeply hurtful. Yes I know. Now, the Grand Remonstrance...'

I still have all my old WGS reports and looking over the subject comments for the first time in forty-odd years I am astonished and impressed at how well my sixth-form teachers knew me. This level of knowledge made it difficult if not downright impossible for one's youthful indiscretions to escape detection. During one of those long-ago lunchtimes I nipped into the History Room and covered the blackboard with a fanciful family tree which began with a caveman called Pop-Ur and included rather better known historical luminaries such as Populius Caesar, Popilliam the Skirronqueror, Popoleon Skirroparte, Popislas Skirrovinsky, an 18th-century king of Popland and of course Worriks the Kingmaker. Mr Skirrow, entering the room for our first class of the afternoon, regarded my creation impassively for a moment before swivelling round and scanning our expectant ranks.

'Very amusing, Taylor. Now, gentlemen, the Heads of Proposals…'

The amalgamation of WGS with the Thomas Linacre School was presumably intended, among other objectives, to address a demographic imbalance between the two schools, for during the year leading up to it our sixth form was evidently quite sorely pressed for accommodation, which is why we had to have some of our History classes in the crypt. The current WGS building dated only from 1936 so any idea the Reader may be forming of a cobweb-festooned Gothic catacomb will be quite erroneous. The crypt was simply a small, dark, poky ground-level storeroom beneath the tower, filled to bursting point with wobbly desks and chairs rejected from more salubrious classrooms. It had one small window high up in a wall and as there were no radiators the caretaker had installed a gas fire controlled with two chains which hung down, one on each side of it. In the 'normal' position, which was really all that was required in such a confined and stuffy space, the gas fire burbled quietly to itself in the background, but when the 'boost' chain was pulled it sprang into life with a surprisingly loud 'bang!' and 'whoosh!' The crypt gas fire clearly had dramatic possibilities, especially as we knew that our European history course was rapidly approaching 1815 and the Battle of Waterloo.

Came the great day and Wellington surveyed his troops with sardonic pride: 'I don't know what they'll do to the French, but by God they frighten me.' Then cannons boomed, muskets rattled, chargers neighed and Congreve's rockets wrought screaming havoc in their own ranks as much as in those of the enemy. Hougoumont was stormed and the Old Guard made its final desperate charge as Von Blücher's Prussians arrived in the nick of time to save the day. Pop, at the height of his histrionic powers, and with the light of battle in his eye, could of course

Candyman/Bigstock

have tackled the Grand Army single-handed and brought about the nemesis of the Corsican tyrant with one hand looped over his head, but we had thoughtfully provided him with reinforcements. Operated from the back row by Barry Lown, via two pieces of clothes line attached to its chains and run discreetly under the desks down each side of the room, the crypt gas fire banged and whooshed throughout the conflict.

And was Mr Skirrow distracted by Barry's antics with the gas fire? Was he f... not a bit of it. In fact, he was so absorbed in the conflict that I don't believe he even noticed the assorted sound effects and noises off.

Mrs Skirrow hailed from Edinburgh and her husband's 'Vale' in the Summer 1964 magazine spoke of the couple's intention to remove to Scotland, but when, some months after Pop's retirement, Gordon Parr and I visited them in their Edwardian semi in Wigan's leafy Spencer Road, we saw no sign of removal or even packing.

'You'll be looking forward to settling back into Edinburgh, then, Mrs Skirrow.'

'Indeed we are, are we not, Philip?' she replied in her genteel Morningside accent.

Pop regarded us impassively. 'Possibly... eventually,' he replied. A keen member of the local Field Club, he enjoyed an active retirement and died just short of his eightieth birthday having successfully postponed the threatened move for more than fourteen happy years.

Christmas Day In Hospital

From *A Wigan Childhood* by John Sharrock Taylor

I was no more than four at the time and I retain only a vague impression of the yellow ambulance, the red blankets and the kindly ambulance men. At the Royal Albert Edward Infirmary in Wigan Lane my mother and I were put into a single room and my silver-painted bed was covered with a transparent plastic oxygen tent. I must have felt better almost immediately because I caught sight of the steel cylinders standing upright nearby and asked my male nurse: 'What are those things?'

'They're little men who are going to help you breathe better.'

I suppose I must eventually have slept, though I doubt if my mother did as she sat in a hard chair by my bedside. The room was at the front of the building, quite close to the casualty department, and it seems to me that for a long time I tranquilly watched the lights of the ambulances tracking backwards and forwards across the ceiling. Penicillin was the new wonder drug and I responded rapidly to it, though I did not enjoy the frequent intramuscular injections. As soon as my breathing stabilised I was shifted into Upper Johnson Ward which was full of other children and it was there, strange to relate, that I spent one of the most enjoyable Christmases of my life.

The ward was festooned with brightly coloured decorations and we played party games such as 'Pass the Parcel'. Nurses in starched caps and blue, red-lined capes came to sing carols and when Sister wasn't looking they and the younger doctors involved themselves in a rather incomprehensible ritual involving a sprig of mistletoe. On Christmas Day visiting hours were relaxed and parents arrived with armfuls of presents. Beatrice and Bill, understandably choked with emotion that their only child had to spend Christmas in hospital, were dumbfounded when I thanked them politely for their gifts and told them they could go home. With typical childish callousness I was having fun with my friends and did not wish to be interrupted.

My parents' particular present was much more than an armful. It was an Austin Pathfinder pedal racing car, with the swept tail characteristic of the real racers of that era, and in all respects it was superior to every other pedal car I have ever seen. The bodywork was pressed from the same heavy-gauge steel Austin used in their road cars and painted to the same standard. The detachable curved bonnet was held in place by two thick leather straps and the wheels had proper track-rods and real pneumatic tyres with deep tread. Even the engine looked convincing, with genuine spark plugs and a distributor. All in all, this masterpiece had only one defect, which was soon to emerge.

Christmas is not Christmas without a tree and that year Upper Johnson Ward had a beauty, standing about twelve feet high, with dense, glossy dark green foliage and the classic fat pyramidal Christmas tree shape. It had been lovingly decorated by the nurses with tinsel, coloured glass baubles and cotton wool snow, and from its pinnacle a golden angel with a trumpet gazed down the length of the ward. My racing car had caused a lot of interest among the other children and we took it in turns to pedal up and down the ward, though we soon discovered that with three or four pushers we could reach a much higher speed than with one child pedalling. The problem was that the Austin was not really intended to travel fast and its brakes were almost non-existent. Seated in the cockpit and fancying myself as Stirling Moss, I egged on my team to new heights of daring. The ward, which looked long from our childish height, proved shorter than we had bargained for. The car struck the Christmas tree head-on and for a moment it hung poised at an angle before it crashed down, enveloping us in swathes of tinsel and scratchy conifer-scented branches. Ornaments smashed, ricocheted and rolled in all directions. The ward door stood open and I believe one of the baubles even ended up in Lower Johnson Ward. This was the end of motoring as far as the Infirmary was concerned and when my embarrassed parents arrived for their next visit they were firmly instructed to take the Austin home with them.

CHAPTER 14

LUVVIES, FLOOZIES AND FLIVVERS

As a chat-up line it made a change from 'What do you do for a living?' Val has always been less than comfortable with luvvies, so after-show parties could be something of a chore. The lavish get-together after the last night at Wigan Little Theatre of John Whiting's *The Devils*, in which I had greatly enjoyed playing the psychopathic exorcist Father Barré, was a case in point.

'Why do they call everybody "darling"?'

'Probably because most of them can't stand each other.'

If vanity (mine, I'm afraid, not hers) had persuaded my young wife to make the best of her beautiful eyes by keeping those 1960s flyaway specs in her handbag, that myopic stare down a naturally imperious nose could be unintentionally intimidating.

'Er, you mentioned that you drive to work. What car do you have?'

'A Dennis.'

'What? You drive a fire engine?'

Val's personal transportation was not, of course, anything of the kind. She had christened her diminutive red 1954 Austin A30 in honour of Major Dennis Bloodnok (Indian Army, Coward and Bar) of *Goon Show* fame.

Over the years I too have flirted with some mature charmers and had full-blown affairs with not a few of them. And most of them also had pet names. Whenever a new mistress hove into view I would tell my long-suffering wife, 'Think yourself lucky. Some men waste their money on floozies rather than flivvers.'

My love affairs with classic and not-so-classic cars started when I was in single figures and living with my parents at 272 Warrington Road in Ince. Just before the winter dawn I would wake and come to sudden and complete consciousness, as I do now sixty years later. Perhaps passing headlights – in my memory they belong always to one of the first British streamlined cars, the Austin A40 Devon – would track across the ceiling

Dennis Bloodnok aka Val's red 1954 Austin A30   *Urbanbuzz/ Shutterstock*

and I would lie in bed and imagine myself behind the wheel of such a wonderful machine. Many years later I bought my only Devon from a Lancaster chef who told me solemnly, 'This car once belonged to the man who invented the croquette potato.'

As I have already mentioned, the first vehicle I ever owned was an Austin Pathfinder pedal car with which I devastated the Christmas tree in Upper Johnson Ward at the Royal Albert Edward Infirmary. When my granddaughter Jaya was at the sturdily toddling age, I trawled the Internet with the idea of vicariously revisiting my childhood by buying her a Pathfinder. I ought to have been (but wasn't) prepared to discover that a good example now fetches around £4,000. In fact, one can find a very decent Dennis for rather less money.

There have been a number of times in my life when my weakness for classic cars has collided with one of my other great failings, inveterate nosiness. When I was in my early teens we lived for a time on the corner of Bradshaw Street and Whelley. The big Victorian house just across the main road, three-storey and high-gabled in red Accrington brick, was occupied by an older lady and an attractive dark-haired daughter, who I suppose would have been in her thirties. Every evening a well-dressed gentleman in a smart suit and a brown trilby would pick her up in an immaculate blue Ford V8 Pilot. They would return very late at night and sit talking in the car often until well after midnight. Then the lady would re-enter the house and the car would slide away down the hill without the driver using the starter. I was curious but probably too young to put two and two together to make four – and if I had done so the result would have been five, because when I finally mentioned it to my parents, my father (brought up in Whelley) told me: 'The gentleman is a well-known Wigan solicitor and the lady is his wife.' According to my Dad they lived in separate houses because of some eccentricity of the mother, but saw each other almost every evening.

It was while we were living in our two-up-two-down in Bradshaw Street with its uneven floors and outside lavatory that my grandfather's brother, great-uncle Jeff, came to visit us from Connecticut. Quiet, smiling, Jeff was the complete antithesis of the rich, loud insensitive American returnee of British legend but I was desperately conscious of the huge economic gulf between the two sides of my family. Already fascinated by cars, I quickly extracted from Jeff that he drove a Chrysler New Yorker sedan in not one but two shades of metallic green. It was of course automatic, and had a huge V8 engine, two-tone leather upholstery, whitewall tyres, electric windows and tinted glass. In contrast, my father had a 1955 sit-up-and-beg Ford Popular, which, I defensively maintained to Jeff, was far superior in quality to tinny, flashy Yankee creations.

'Show me,' said Jeff tolerantly and I led him to the 'backs' behind the house. He gazed impassively at our diminutive fawn 'Pop' with its 1930s styling and red rexine upholstery.

'Lift the hood.'

'Don't you mean the bonnet?'

'Lift it.'

Uncle Jeff stood for a moment regarding the quasi-antique squat, square 1172cc side-valve engine.

'Is that the motor?'

175

'Yes.'

'My generator's as big as that.'

I can still remember the excitement of driving my first powered vehicle: that feeling of being barely in control of something which seemed to have an unpredictable life of its own. When I was fifteen I owned a share in a 1936 Morris Eight which my friends and I drove untaxed, uninsured and totally illegally in the country lanes near Haigh. It went well but had a tendency towards the palsy because of worn kingpins. We bought it for seven pounds ten from a fly-by-night dealer on one of the slum-clearance lots down Prescot Street, where the air was richly perfumed by Gallaghers' glue factory. It was a fascinating area, full of multi-coloured pre-war wrecks with bald tyres, mildewed upholstery and sagging springs, and when I later read Steinbeck's *The Grapes of Wrath* it all came flooding vividly back to me.

Shortly after the syndicated Morris had given up the ghost I turned seventeen, and decided to buy an E-Type – and I knew exactly where one could be had for twenty-five quid. Now, I should explain that the part-exchange vehicle I had seen standing on the forecourt of James Berry's Foxfield Garage wasn't a Jaguar E-Type but a 1939 Series E, a slightly later Morris Eight than our previous model.

With his natty pinstripes and toothbrush moustache Mr Berry was the image of the sharp operator, but there the resemblance ended. He flirted decorously with my girlfriend Audrey and got down to business.

'Twenty-five pounds, young people, is just the start. Are you working yet.'

'No, we're still at school.'

'I thought so. Petrol's five bob a gallon. Have you thought about insurance?'

'Er, no.'

'I thought not. Well, it's compulsory, and for a seventeen-year-old on a provisional licence it isn't cheap.'

'We could wait to insure the car until we've saved up a bit more.'

'So you'd need to garage it, or at least park it off the street.'

'My Dad has a garage.'

'What does he keep in there at the moment?'

'His car.'

'I thought so. Listen, children, I'm going to do you a big favour...'

'Oh, thank you...'

'And not sell you a car.'

I may have had Mr Berry's strictures in mind during my first term at Lancaster University when I finally got round to purchasing my first independent motorised transportation, an NSU Prima scooter which cost very little to insure and went for miles on an eggcupful of two-stroke mixture. But it was a Spartan mode of travel, especially through the cold winter of 1964–5. With a top speed of 40 mph on the flat, dropping steeply to 15 on any kind of gradient, a home visit to Wigan was an odyssey not to be taken lightly, especially as I had to do the whole thing on the winding A6 and A49 roads, L drivers being banned from the newly opened M6 Preston by-pass.

With snow on the fells I set out across the Pennines to visit my schoolmate Gordon Parr, who had just started his History degree at Leeds. I was wearing thick gloves and almost every stitch of clothing I possessed, but when I stopped in Ilkley for a cup of coffee my hands were so numb that it took me fully five minutes to undo the toggles of my duffel coat.

I literally swopped the NSU for a tidy little grey Standard 8 saloon which had been registered in 1946, the year of my birth. She flagged dismally on hills until it occurred to me to replace her fuel pump. (My college friend Michael Caddock had claimed to be deeply humiliated the day we were stormed past by a Dukinfield Corporation bus). But it was on Morecambe promenade that I had my first encounter with the Stalwart Guardians of the Law.

'Mike, there's an idiot right on my tail, flashing his headlights in the rear-view mirror. I'm going to step on it and lose the bugger.'

Like the voice of God, the instruction seemed to come from a disapproving sky: 'Car number MMF 160, pull into the side, please!'

It is strange that I still remember that registration plate after more than four decades, because I would struggle to tell you the number of the Ford I have been driving for the last ten years. It seemed that the 'nods' habitually targeted us students, which was hardly surprising as we were usually doing something illegal and we tended to drive vehicles which combined great antiquity with astounding decrepitude. And the second question (the one which came after 'Do you know what speed you were doing in a 30 mph zone?') was always: 'Can you tell me the registration number of this vehicle?'

'No, but if I were going to nick a car do you really think I'd have chosen this one?'

The Standard was reliable and economical to run, so common sense dictated eternal faithfulness, but in love affairs my heart has always ruled my head. And Mephistopheles was one of the few thoroughly masculine vehicles to whom I have ever given that most susceptible of organs. The near-immaculate black 1936 Riley Nine Merlin sports saloon, with its midnight blue leather interior, stood in an alleyway in Lancaster's Scotforth suburb. Noting the 'For Sale' sign I duly banged on a back gate and summoned the owner.

'I should warn you that I've already had an offer for it.'

'How much?'

'Twelve pounds.'

'Would fifteen be acceptable?'

'Done.'

The twin-overhead-cam power unit ran with a deep burble which seemed to confirm Mephistopheles's infernal credentials. Like all the Rileys of his era he was fitted with a preselect gearbox, a lever on the steering column which allowed the driver to pre-programme his next gear change and complete it with a light tap of the foot. For the competition Rileys such as the Imp or the Gamecock this might have given a split second's advantage, but on the much slower Merlin I couldn't really see the point of it, though the unit counterpointed the engine noise with rather an interesting whine. The doyen of the 1930s road Rileys was the low-slung, elegantly aerodynamic Kestrel Sprite. With a much more efficient power—weight ratio and the same huge nineteen inch 'knock-on' wheels as the Merlin, it could see off quite a few of the middle-range sports cars of the 1960s and I felt a thrill of pride when one of these thoroughbreds saluted Mephistopheles with a cheerful flash of its P100 headlights on the A49 near Euxton one misty Sunday morning.

By now the Reader will have gathered that I am a thoroughly faithless lover, so it will come as no surprise that my first sight of the Land-

The Land-Going Speedboat aka my 1948 Triumph Roadster   *Media Digital Pro/*
Shutterstock

Going-Speed-Boat left me gasping for breath. My fellow Lancaster undergraduate Graham Nunn, about whom more in a moment, was responsible for the strange name. The black 1948 Triumph Roadster was exactly the same model as the one later to be the chosen transportation of Sergeant Bergerac, the TV detective. She suffered from dodgy brakes and wandering steering but the bodywork, interior and hood were near perfect, and I had to have her. Her owner, another undergraduate, couldn't afford the repairs. Neither could I but I somehow scraped the overdraft together.

Apart from old cars and young women, my other great Lancaster enthusiasm was debating, and I travelled quite long distances to indulge it. Shortly after I acquired the Land-Going-Speed-Boat I was scheduled to appear in a competition at Hull University with my debating partner Ken Todd, and we had arranged to pick up Gordon Parr from Leeds on the way. It was another raw January day with deep snow on the Pennines. The Triumph's single bench seat would accommodate three at a pinch but she also had an open 'dickey' in the boot with its own fold-up windscreen, and we thought Gordon, swathed in rugs and wearing a woolly hat and my flying-jacket, would do very well there. Arriving in Hull we had to lift him out because he was frozen into a sitting position.

Graham Nunn was a Lancaster character who hid a keen intelligence under a zany appearance. Graham's mum was an East End gal and his dad was a Cockney butcher who looked exactly like a Cockney butcher. Graham, their only child, was a young Spike Milligan with a huge beard, wild hair and an even wilder voice. No son could have been more diametrically different from his parents and they loved him to bits. I have been known to claim, not entirely convincingly, that while supposedly reading for my BA I sacrificed the chance of a first-class degree to the demands of my various mechanical mistresses, and the adventure I shared with Graham was a case in point. After an extremely patchy three years at university I ought to have been cramming for my finals, but browsing *Exchange and Mart*, the flivver fancier's vade-mecum, I came across an advert for a 1939 MG TA sports roadster which was for sale in Southport at the very attractive price of thirty pounds. By now you will readily understand that I didn't actually have thirty quid but my long-suffering bank had always been accommodating. In any case I was now on the threshold of paid employment and I was confident that the gnomes of Lancaster would again supply the necessary. So Graham and I set out for Southport in a spirit of adventure and anticipation. The red MG turned out to be complete and reasonably tidy. I already knew that it was a non-runner so we hitched it up with a tow rope to the back of the Triumph. This kind of towing is fraught with danger and nowadays it is understandably illegal. The MG's brake pads were down to the rivets so we took it steady, with me carefully signalling all intended manoeuvres and Graham keeping the rope as taught as possible.

All went well until we reached the long, steep hill at Fulwood on the Southport side of Preston. There were traffic lights at the bottom of the slope and about two hundred yards before the Triumph reached them they turned red. I didn't have the option of 'running' the lights because traffic with priority was already beginning to cross the junction, so I tried to brake as smoothly as I possibly could. Glancing fearfully in the rear-view mirror I saw a vehicle about to overtake me. As you have probably guessed, it was a red MG TA roadster. Fortunately there was nothing approaching us from the opposite direction. The laws of geometry operated and as the MG passed me at some speed it described a precise arc and ended up facing me head-on at the end of the bar-taut tow rope. In some trepidation I left the Triumph and peered in under the MG's tatty canvas hood.

'Are you all right, Graham?'

Wild eyes glittered out of an impenetrable mass of barnet and beard, then: 'It's bloody hairy in here, you know!'

I emerged from college life into the harsh glare of the real world armed with the inevitable 'Desmond', and took up my first teaching post at my alma mater, Wigan Grammar School. The Edwardian masher traditionally invited the young maiden to come upstairs and see his etchings but my invitation to Val, a few weeks later after a rehearsal of *The Gondoliers*, was rather different: 'Come to Sunday tea and meet Ruby.'

There must have been few occasions in the history of romance when a man has taken a girl home to meet his current inamorata, but this was one of them. Ruby, of course, was my 1936 Austin Seven. When I had discovered her in a derelict, leaking garage in a 'backs' off Greenough Street she had been quietly rotting unused for fifteen years. The nearside bodywork was badly rusted and both sills were completely shot but, incredibly, when we pumped up the tyres they held air. The engines of badly-stored vehicles are often seized solid but the 750cc sidevalve turned easily on the starting handle. A gallon of Shellmex and a new battery and she started with a throaty roar.

I spent much of my spare time in the next six months cleaning and scraping. Every oil gasket was leaking and this proved to be a blessing in disguise because the underside of the car was coated with thick black gunk, and when I cleaned this off with paraffin I found a perfect chassis underneath. Much of the cotton-sheathed wiring was also soaked in oil and the electrics were consequently hit-and-miss. Being clueless in such matters, I solved the problem piecemeal, carefully tracing and removing each wire in turn then replacing it with new. To renew the gaskets and sort out the erratic clutch the engine had to come out. Removing the whole bonnet assembly, I unbolted the gearbox and the engine mountings, whose rubbers, soaked in oil, would also have to be replaced. At this point I was stymied because the garage of our family home at

17 Sandringham Close in Pemberton had no hoist. As I pondered the problem, my mother Beatrice arrived with a mug of tea. I had thought of gradually jacking up the engine block, balancing it on bricks and then simply pushing the car backwards away from the power unit but Mum, a former swimming teacher with powerful upper torso muscles, simply stepped over a main chassis member, embraced the engine and lifted it clear in one fluid movement. She put on a formidable Lancashire Sunday tea and all.

Ruby was fun but hardly practical for day to day transport, so we made an assignation via the motor ads page of the *Manchester Evening News* and met Emilia in a back street in Moss Side. The scruffy black 1954 Rover 75's largely aluminium bodywork was grimy and dull but perfect apart from the rusty steel rear quarter panels and battered radiator louvres. The mahogany dashboard and door fitments were largely unmarked but the cloth interior was stained and ragged. She started on the button and the engine purred. Forty quid changed hands and we drove her home. She was fifth-hand and the buff log book showed that the original owner had been a lady called Emilia and that was that.

A remarkably modest investment in cash and a rather more lavish one in time and effort restored Emilia to much of her original glory. A breaker's yard supplied replacement quarter panels and a complete and sumptuous green leather interior from a write-off Rover 100. Half a litre of T-Cut and a great deal of elbow grease brought the bodywork up to a pristine shine. Her immediate predecessor had been an Austin Healey 'frogeye' Sprite, and a six-foot-five-inch friend who had been unable to get his knees under the froggy's low dashboard luxuriated in Emilia's cavernous interior: 'How many funerals has it done?'

Not long after Emilia returned from having her 'new' quarter panels painted, we drove over on a winter Friday evening to spend the weekend at 12 Milton Grove with Val's mother Ethel and Aunt Winnie. We left the M6 and a hundred yards after the Orrell exit I indicated, moved to the crown of the road and waited for a gap in the oncoming traffic prior to making the right turn into Shelley Drive. Fortunately, seat belts were by then compulsory. Emilia's huge, supportive front seats and massive chassis, irreparably bent by the impact, saved us from more serious injury than the inevitable whiplash, but the white Ford Anglia which had ploughed into us at speed from behind was totally demolished from the windscreen forward. As they loaded the driver into the ambulance she muttered painfully: 'I was admiring your car.'

Since those far off times there have been other loves in my life including at one time a small harem of P4 Rovers, some of which actually went, but these days life on the high road is a lot less varicoloured than it was when Mephistopheles burbled along the A49 past Lil's Caff. Our grey Ford Fusion has carried Val and me around the Iberian Peninsula for ten years and 170,000 safe, economical and trouble-free kilometres but (whisper it not in Gathurst, tell it not in the streets of Aspull) she is just a bit, well, boring. From time to time, in a spirit of masochistic nostalgia, I browse the classic car websites. Mephistopheles and his brothers now fetch £20,000 and upwards and so does a pristine example of the Land-Going-Speedboat, but decent Dennises and Rubies can be had for a quarter of that sum. Perhaps, just one last time...

Getting It Right

A self-made entrepreneur (could it have been Dave Whelan?) was inspired to set up an erotic supermarket in a redundant branch of Tesco. As he worked on the details of the project the phrase that popped into his mind was 'horses (or at least fillies) for courses', and he decided to be very precise in targeting the various socio-economic groups of potential customers. On the ground floor, exorbitantly expensive, were the super-models; on the first floor the 'celebritees' with which the media is so besotted; on the next floor, the soap actresses, and so on. On the very top floor, definitely cut price, were the teachers.

After a couple of months the entrepreneur reviewed his takings and was horrified to discover that all the different departments were losing money hand over fist, with the single exception of the teachers, who were absolutely coining it in. He rushed round to his super bordello and, listening at a ground floor door, was distressed to hear a rather tense female voice saying: 'Try not to mess up my makeup but DO hurry up and get it over with. I'm out of the cathouse and on to the catwalk in less than ten minutes.'

It was the same story on almost every floor. The actresses would only countenance positions in which they could continue studying their lines. The nuns in particular put their customers off their stroke by clicking their rosary beads at all the wrong moments. Beryl, the fiancée of Bob the Builder, reduced her client to complete incompetence by constantly referring to the mighty power of her live-in lover's JCB.

Finally, having taken the lift to the very top floor, the entrepreneur listened at the door of one of the teachers. There was a long pause and a great deal of heavy breathing. Then a female voice said with studied patience: 'Listen, I don't care how many times we do this, or how much it costs you, but you're not going home until you get it RIGHT.'

CHAPTER 15

MINING BUTTY

When I was fifteen I fell in love with a girl of the same age with the face of a Murillo madonna. She was called Audrey, and I have described in *A Wigan Childhood* how we first met at the youth club in the basement below Wigan's Queen's Hall Methodist Mission.

On this first occasion I had taken the bus from my outlying suburb down to the Market Place, and then walked slowly in spite of the grey chill with my overcoat collar turned up against the rain. Friends from school had encouraged me to join the club but, though not timid, I was bleakly apprehensive at any prospect of meeting strangers in numbers. I particularly distrusted those of my own age who would probably play ping-pong and 'dig' Beatles numbers and who, before they had got the message that verbally I was more than capable of demolishing most, if not all opposition, might be disposed to mock either my reserved and conservative style or my taste for tailored suits and fancy waistcoats.

I paused uncertainly at the top of the wide flight of stairs which led down to the unknown. There was a vaguely ecclesiastical smell compounded equally of polish, dust, disinfectant and old hymn books. At the foot of the staircase two girls stood talking in a pool of bright light which spilled from the open door of a side room. One of them, though she was pretty, I merely registered as unimportant stage dressing. The other was slim, shapely, compact,

Audrey

in a short, slightly flared skirt, medium high heels and a dusty-pink mohair cardigan worn open over a white Peter Pan blouse sprinkled with blue forget-me-nots. A heart-shaped face was framed in a mass of coarse chestnut waves which shone glossily in the side-lighting. She was completely unconscious of my existence and I had the immediate and totally ridiculous sensation that I loved her. Later, when I knew her, I came to understand that for me the special piquancy of her attraction came at least in part from the harmony of contrasts I had perceived in this first moment of seeing her. It was both physical and spiritual, but initially I was conscious only of the physical: her hair was rough-textured, coarser than I have ever known in any other human being, rich in colour and to the touch exactly like an Airedale's coat. Her dark brows were heavy over eyes which reflected the forget-me-not blue of that first blouse. She was slim and small-breasted but her little hands were square and practical, her calves sturdy, muscular and well-shaped like an Italian peasant girl's, her features small and fine-boned, her complexion white satin tinged with rose which died to a faint half-flush along her throat. I do not remember hearing her voice on this first occasion. Afterwards, when I knew its sound well, I came to identify it with the rich chestnut of her hair. Though never loud it was a deep, slightly throaty contralto. Audrey was a fourth-form pupil at the Girls' High School and her speech, like my own, was consciously more attuned to the middle-class norm than to the south Lancashire working class. Like myself she loved music but she was one of the few people I have met in my life who genuinely could not sing in tune. When eventually we arrived at a relationship which would allow this without embarrassment, I tried to teach her to imitate simple musical phrases. Though she would occasionally manage to do so, she would prove quite incapable of repeating the feat half a minute later. In church, supported by the organ and the other voices, she managed the hymns at tenor pitch, only slightly off-key. I think this intractable tone-deafness would have irritated me profoundly in any other human being. In her it was only an endearing blemish in someone otherwise perfect.

Audrey's maternal grandfather was a baritone who had sung her to sleep with Paul Robeson's lullaby 'My Curly-Headed Baby'. His name was Emmanuel Lovekin and Audrey thought the name came from

Staffordshire. Her grandmother Annie told me that her father-in-law, born in Tunstall in 1864, had also been an Emmanuel Lovekin and a singer. 'He was a big strapping man who sang in a high tenor,' she recalled, 'a voice like a baby.' Thirty years on I searched for the name on the Internet and discovered that there had been an even earlier Emmanuel Lovekin, Audrey's great-great-grandfather, a self-made man who had made his own distinctive mark on the industrial history of the Potteries. This Emmanuel wrote his autobiography when he was almost seventy-five years old and in quoting from it I shall not interrupt the flow by showing where I have edited his words. If you want to read the original text, I have included the details in the Acknowledgements at the end of this book.

Emmanuel Lovekin was born at Donnington in Shropshire in 1820. His father Thomas was a furnace man in an iron foundry and earned good money, but he took little interest in the family and spent most of his earnings on drink. According to Emmanuel it was his mother Sinah who controlled their nine children with a masterly hand. The infant Emmanuel was sent to a dame's school run by an elderly Primitive Methodist lady called Tilly Wilson. Nineteenth-century Methodists had a no-nonsense attitude towards sin, and Tilly stood the infants on a bench and taught them a song which went:

O ye youngsters be not proud
For ye must die and wear a shroud.

Methodism was originally a movement within the Church of England, and its founders, John and Charles Wesley, were Anglican priests to their dying day. The Methodists were so called because they approached their religion seriously and methodically, unlike many clergy of the established church, who were clearly less interested in Jesus than in glebes, tithes, huntin', shootin' and fishin'. Just count up the vicars in the novels of Jane Austen and Anthony Trollope, then make a note of any who actually mention God, and you will know exactly where the Methodists were coming from. Above all, Methodism was a working-class movement with a biblical emphasis on social justice. Its great preachers held vast open-air meetings and hundreds of thousands of ordinary people who had felt no connection with religion were converted and baptised. In early 19th century England, as Hogarth's trenchant cartoons vividly show, it was not religion but cheap gin that was the opiate of the people. Methodism set its face firmly against the demon drink and in middle age Emmanuel would dissolve a lucrative business partnership because the other party refused to get rid of his ale house.

As a child I was puzzled by the term Primitive Methodist. Did the congregations dress in skins like cartoon cavemen? Did assegais thump into the pulpit whenever the preacher droned on for too long or wandered off the subject? Later I understood that their primitivism was simply an attempt to get back to the original purity of the movement, which was being diluted by middle-class notions of respectability. Emmanuel Lovekin was to become an employer, a Sunday school superintendent and a respected figure in his community, but his lifelong championship of the working class and the disadvantaged continued throughout his long life.

At seven, Emmanuel's formal education, such as it was, stopped short when he was sent to work in a coal mine. In 1827 there was scant regard for health and safety, but one precaution mine owners did take was to install doors at various points to help contain fires and explosions. Emmanuel's first job below ground was to open these doors to let the wagons pass along the 'roads' between the coal face and the mineshaft. When his younger brother took over the door-keeping Emmanuel was promoted to driving a donkey. At thirteen, his thigh was badly broken in a pit accident. In those days, long before such fractures were routinely pinned, the principal treatment was to lie still with the femur immobilised with sandbags. But boredom and inactivity had their compensations and Emmanuel later wrote: 'I had to lie in bed for thirteen weeks and began to feel strongly the desire to read and write. Friends came to read to me and when I was able I went to a night school.' He adds self-deprecatingly: 'The schoolmaster was a very good violin player and I began to learn too. I scratched for many years but could never make much of it.'

Like many children of nonconformist families, Emmanuel received his real education in Sunday school where, he says modestly, 'I learned to read fairly well and write a bit'. In his early twenties 'things were very bad with little work and very little money for it'. It was a time of great political ferment, not only in Britain but in mainland Europe, where revolutions broke out and monarchies toppled throughout the 1840s. In England the protectionist Corn Laws, which kept food prices artificially high, were strongly opposed by both industrialists and their employees and, being literate, Emmanuel was elected Secretary of his local Chartist club. Feelings ran high and he records attending a meeting of 30,000 people on the Wrekin. Sometimes the protests boiled over into violence and in attempting to contain one such riot Emmanuel was arrested and indicted for 'conspiring to raise the rate of wages', an offence punishable by transportation to Australia, as in the case of the Tolpuddle Martyrs. The court acquitted him, and suspecting one of his so-called friends of being a police informer, he resolved to be more careful about the company he kept in the future.

There was little satisfaction in working down a coal pit at half a crown a day, and at the age of twenty-three Emmanuel and a friend set out to tramp the Midlands in search of employment. The early Victorian railway boom was in full swing. There was plenty of tunnelling work to be had and the two friends also quarried stone for the new locks on the Stourport–Worcester section of the Severn navigation. They made good money but saved little as they lived well and were always restless to be on the move.

In 1843 Emmanuel's wanderings ceased when he returned to Tunstall and married a girl called Edna Simcock. 'I never repented of the act,' he wrote, 'and we lived happily for thirty-six years until death parted us in 1881'. In fact, Emmanuel's experience of marriage had been so positive that in 1882 he wed Harriet Lowe, thirteen years his junior, a marriage which endured up to his death at the age of eighty-five in 1905.

After his marriage to Edna, Emmanuel had embarked on his main career. A mining 'butty' was a contractor who undertook to sink new pits on behalf of investors, and Emmanuel and his team started many such mines in south Staffordshire. Following the Act of 1872 he obtained his *Colliery Manager's Certificate of Technical Proficiency*, and was invited to manage a number of mines on behalf of their owners. Mining was even more perilous then that it is now, and he and his men quite literally suffered many ups, downs and near fatal accidents. His continuing commitment to social justice led him into some unexpected places. In 1883, the Liberal-controlled Hanley town council espoused the cause of women's suffrage and the following year Emmanuel sponsored a public meeting at the Town Hall with activists Eva McLaren and Alice Scatcherd. Clearly both he and they were thirty years ahead of their time.

Emmanuel and Edna had fourteen children, ten of whom survived to raise families of their own, and his seven-thousand-word autobiographical sketch includes a brief review of the progress of a few of them. Poor William, 'the black sheep of the family', is widowed and has taken to drink. John and James and their families are in Philadelphia. When they left England for the last time they can hardly have expected to see their father again, but in 1887 he set sail from Liverpool for a four-month visit to his descendants in the New World. Emmanuel (the tenor) is established in Wigan and is already the father of Emmanuel (the future baritone) who in turn would be the grandfather of Audrey, my first love.

Being in love did not guarantee that love was requited. Audrey was friendly towards me from the first but at fifteen she was her father's girl, a cherished only child who was happily absorbed in school work and family rituals. She had a particular friend, Christine, with whom I had seen her talking on that first occasion, and who monopolised her leisure hours. I also had a friend, James, who, I thought craftily, could be persuaded to occupy Christine's attention while I made some much-needed progress with Audrey. Years later, when she was the headmistress of an Anglican girls' school, Audrey's pupils asked her if she had had a boyfriend while at school. 'Yes I did,' she replied, 'and we used to meet in the rose garden of Mesnes Park almost every afternoon after classes.' Indeed we did, and like generations of Wigan youngsters we would sometimes invite good luck by rubbing the shoe of 'th' mon i'th' park', the brooding bronze statue of Sir Francis Sharp Powell, the borough's long-serving Victorian MP.

After 'going out' together for several years, Audrey and I, in some ways too much alike, eventually went our separate ways and found our soul mates in gentler partners than ourselves. She and her husband

Charles have long lived in Australia, while after years of travelling the world Val and I live contentedly in the hills of Andalucía. James and Christine still live in Wigan and, like us, have been happily married for well over forty years.

Writing in October 1902, Emmanuel Lovekin muses: 'We have had a lot of rainy weather and I dare not go out. I don't get out to the night meetings now but I am glad I did a bit when I was younger. I feel fairly well but feebly at times. Mrs is nearly seventy and me eighty-three, so we are good for our time and very thankful to God for his care of us through all the days that are past. We will trust him further. We are in good hands.'

Keepin' Thi Cheers A-Whom

Like my wife Val, my cousin Lavinia was brought up in Orrell. 'Orrell near Wigan,' says Val. 'Orrell near Southport,' says Lavinia. For those readers unfamiliar with South-West Lancashire, let me explain that the township of Orrell isn't really peripatetic. I've observed it quite closely over the past sixty-odd years and I can confidently assure you that it stays pretty well in the same spot, which happens to be about three miles west of Wigan Pier. Southport is on the coast, about nineteen miles further along the line from Gathurst station, where Val used to catch the train in the days when the nuns at Birkdale Convent were attempting to turn her into a young lady, though her tendency to hang upside down from the luggage rack while displaying her non-regulation knickers to the awestruck commuting public indicates that this was something of an uphill task.

The main point, as you certainly realised before the end of my third sentence, is that Lavinia thought 'near Southport' was a classier address

Butter wouldn't melt: my future wife in Convent uniform

than 'near Wigan'. Lately she seems to have abandoned the theme and I'd guess that she finds 'Southport Merseyside' something of a comedown.

I have a degree in English and I taught it for thirty-eight years. More to the point, when I was at school, back in nineteen-hundred-and-frozen-to-death, they were still learning us proper grammar, so I've always been fairly clear about subject, predicate and all that jazz. Clear, that is, until Lavinia decided to re-educate me.

'The staff presented a crystal bowl to Val and me,' I told her.

'That's wrong.'

'Is it?'

'Of course it is. It should be "The staff presented a crystal bowl to Val and I."'

'So if Val wasn't there it would be "The staff presented a crystal bowl to I"? That there do sound a bit piratical to I, m'dear.'

'Don't be silly.'

'Bear with my silliness for a moment and tell me why you think it should be "Val and I" rather than "Val and me".'

'Because "I" is more polite than "me".'

'I see. Polite. Like leaving a bit of fairy cake on the side of your plate and sticking your little finger out when you drink your tea from a china cup.'

'You're being silly again.'

'Guilty as charged. But let's break the original sentence down into its component parts.

'SUBJECT: The staff

VERB: presented

PREPOSITION: to

DIRECT OBJECT: a crystal bowl

INDIRECT OBJECT: Val and me

'"I" and "me" are pronouns. The subject form of the pronoun is "I". The object form is "me", therefore "The staff presented a crystal bowl to Val and me".'

'It's still wrong.'

'Why?'

'Because I've always said "Val and I".'

'There's no arguing with that.'

Another of Lavinia's assertions that regularly has me grinding my teeth is: 'Wigan has no dialect. Just lazy speech.'

'Lazy? How many facial muscles do you think you'd use if you said "My next-door neighbour is very presumptuous?"'

'I have no idea. Why?'

'I'll guarantee that it's a lot fewer than if you said "Er next doo-er's getten a face as ud stond cloggin". And say "mud" and then savour that lovely Wigan word "slutch".'

'I'll do no such thing.'

The dialect of the Wigan area is a particularly rich mixture of historical influences, though of course it has been watered down by increased mobility and the influence of the mass media. In ancient times we were part of the territory of the Brigantes, fragments of whose Celtic language survive in place names such as Ince, meaning an island in a marshy landscape. And when my mother referred to her brat she wasn't insulting me but using the pure Welsh, and Wigan, word for an apron. When she *was* insulting me for some entirely fancied failure in horse sense she'd call me a gobbin. I only started researching our family history after her death and I sometimes smile to think how amused she'd be to know that I am descended, on my father's side of course, from a certain 16th-century Ann Gobbin.

Vikings and Saxons settled in our area, which is why we can still hear their speech in different versions of the same names, such as Skelmersdale and Shelmerdine. Those *Sk* and *Sh* alternatives are still common in modern speech. Folk elsewhere may shriek but in Wigan we skrike. As you may imagine, my college friend John Skitt came in for some teasing when we covered the topic in an English Language seminar. The bobbies on the old Borough force were all Vikings and even in his seventies retired Sergeant Wood had muscles like Popeye. 'My Joe's still a joton,' said Mrs Wood proudly, using the Old Norse word for 'giant'. And I can still hear my father muttering that there wasn't a skorrock of coal left in the scuttle. He also gave me a lesson in grammatical etiquette which was useful when I was learning French and Spanish:

'Wheer's th 'ommer?'

'I gi'ed it thee.'

'Nay lad, I thous thee but tha doesn't thou me.'

When I was a lad it was possible to identify the differences in accent between villages only a couple of miles apart. The pronunciation of the consonant 'r' can still be a clue and I noticed on a recent visit that while Aspullers 'park the car', Ashtonians, like Bostonians, 'paak the caa'. My great-aunt Polly lived in an old stone weaver's cottage in Daisy Hill, with a steep flight of steps up to the front door. On a hot summer day, when he had been pedalling a heavy bicycle and delivering packages up and down the neighbouring steps, the grocer's lad looked longingly at our laden tea table and said pathetically: 'Ee, Mrs Blundell, my legs are warchin!' Aunt Polly did not extend the desired invitation. Or as my grandmother put it, lapsing into the same dialect: 'Er leet 'em warch.' The speech of those old folks was rich in metaphor. In her eighties Edie, another of my great-aunts, aware that advancing age had trimmed an inch or two off her stately height, told me 'I'll soon be able to walk under th' ess-hole wi' a tall 'at on.' My grandmother had to explain that 'th' ess-hole' was the ash pit under the grate.

Then there are the linguistic mysteries. Who on earth was Icky, th' fire bobby? What did 'By the crin!' really mean? Why did folk say they were going 'up th' Sough'? And why are 'moggies' mice in Wigan, when everywhere else in the English-speaking world they are cats? My great-aunt Margaret also used 'moggy' for little 'wick' things that scurried around microscopically. 'Wick' is derived from Anglo-Saxon 'wicca', which in turn is related to 'witch' and all sorts of other interesting stuff.

When, like thousands of Wiganers, my mother gave birth to me in Billinge Hospital, she probably did not know that her great-grandmother and several generations of her family are buried in St Aidan's churchyard. Trawling *YouTube* I came across a video of two old Billingers talking about a third party. 'E's still getten a' his cheers a-whom,' said one of the speakers approvingly, meaning that the person under discussion had managed to maintain his mental faculties. The phrase has an additional resonance in Billinge, once known for its handmade furniture which still fetches high prices on the antiques market. A Billinger who could keep all his chairs at home was a thrifty chap who had not needed to sell off any of his inheritance.

I've just posted Lavinia's Christmas present to Orrell. Near Southport, of course. It's a second-hand copy of Lynne Truss's witty little bestseller *Eats, Shoots and Leaves*. I particularly want her to study Chapter 4: Airs and Graces.

CHAPTER 16

UNDIVIDED BY A COMMON LANGUAGE

'I was recently on a tour of Latin America, and the only regret I have was that I didn't study Latin harder in school so I could converse with those people.' – Dan Quayle

'You know, Bill, I *like* Americans!'

My friend, William Estes Lyons, regarded me with a faintly ironic smile as we sat down to our pints in the public bar of the Spinner and Bergamot.

'Well, John, I guess you *do* like Americans who read books, play Mozart sonatas and hold season tickets for the Metropolitan Opera, but I'm not convinced that you really know much about the rest.'

Bill, twenty-something years older than my callow twenty-seven, was of course warning me about the pitfalls of generalisation but that's a trap most of us fall into from time to time. We Brits have always made patronising remarks about the insularity of Americans, but wasn't it a British newspaper that ran the headline: 'Fog in the Channel, Continent Cut Off'? And haven't we just compounded that kind of stupidity by voting for Brexit?

Bill was the kind of cosmopolitan American who did all of those things he mentioned that summer evening in my village pub. He played the piano to concert standard and it was a book that brought us together and started a friendship of more than twenty years. I wonder how many of my readers remember *Ring of Bright Water*, Gavin Maxwell's romantic story of his life in a remote house in the highlands of Scotland with his pet otters, Mijbil, Edal and Teko? Before the book was published in 1960, Maxwell, the complex and reclusive grandson of the Earl of Northumberland, had been a struggling travel writer. *Ring* made him a rich man and an instant celebrity. He couldn't cope with either fact and died less than nine years later, worn out by a chaotic series of personal and professional disasters mostly of his own making.

In 1973, when Val and I were on holiday in the highlands, I read *Raven, Seek thy Brother*, the tragic third volume of what came to be known as the *Camusfearna* trilogy after the author's home at Sandaig on the shore of the Sound of Sleat. Deeply moved, I simply had to go and see for myself. Gavin Maxwell had been dead for four years. His house had been destroyed in a fire which had killed his famous otter Edal and I had no idea of what I might find when I arrived at the site. This is part of what I wrote when I returned to our rented cottage in Ardnamurchan:

I came first to Camusfearna on a day of rain, when the leaden sky sat motionless on the ridge of Druimfiachlach and the mist wreathed the dark, unstirring spruces of the forestry estate. Steely cataracts glittered through cloud and spray and here and there primroses gleamed like pale ore. Stopping the car a mile or so beyond Glenelg I asked directions of a mechanic at a roadside garage. His laconic reply, 'Away down that track... a good long walk,' told me I was yet another tiresome tourist and possibly mentally deranged in the bargain, since I was evidently prepared to plunge down two miles of quagmire through drenching woods in a steady downpour in search of a dead writer.

For the first few hundred yards, the path followed the line of a burn that bubbled fitfully among boulders and islands of tussocky grass and then made a sudden feint to the right, cutting through the track. A line of tumbled stepping stones, barely showing their slippery heads above the rushing water, pointed out the way and the road rose more or less intact on the other side. My feet were already soaked and I could feel the rain seeping steadily down my back, so I sloshed across this obstacle with no more than a momentary pause. I found myself in a drenched and desolate terrain where scattered granite outcrops alternated with marsh and mud through every winding of the track as it descended steeply to sea level.

And suddenly the Ring of Bright Water lay below me, hemmed in by the mist and rain, a perfect almost-circular bay with grey waves lapping sullenly on a white shell-sand beach backed by a little fenced meadow of marram grass where a dozen black cattle grazed stolidly. Ahead, a chain of small islands, ghostly in the mist with the Cuillins of Skye a faint outline behind them. To the right, its back to the cliff, a blue-shuttered croft house and a plank bridge across a rushing burn overhung with alder and rowan.

As I gazed at this scene, instantly recognisable from the books, I was suddenly aware that I was not alone. On the far side of the meadow the figure of a man was moving slowly towards me through the mist. A few yards nearer and I had an impression of dark eyes and sunburned skin taut over high cheekbones in an alert and serious face. The green Barbour jacket was dark with rain and a soaked strand of black hair straggled from under a knitted fisherman's cap. The stranger paused and at that moment I realised he had with him an otter on a leash. He stooped and hoisted the animal up to his shoulder where it sat with whiskers twitching and regarded me with a bright unblinking gaze. This was my first meeting with Phoebe and with William Estes Lyons, traveller, musician, architect, ceramicist, raconteur and sometime Hollywood bit-part player.

I had read only two books by Gavin Maxwell and immediately fallen under his melancholy spell. Bill Lyons had read everything the man had ever written and we stood in the pouring rain comparing notes. I felt sure that the garage man would have despised us as a prize pair of romantic idiots. Phoebe the otter clearly felt the same and squeaked in protest.

'If she's going to be wet she likes to be properly wet,' said Bill, 'not this drizzly stuff. Yesterday we got too close to an Orca and he swamped our small boat with his tail. They don't see humans as prey but I was scared that she'd end up as a tasty snack. She couldn't have cared less because she knew he couldn't catch her.'

Bill Lyons was born early in the last century at Holly Springs, Mississippi, to a family that had owned a crumbling antebellum mansion very like the Tara of *Gone with the Wind*. His great-granduncle, an officer in the army of the South, had been wounded at Gettysburg, and until his beautiful mother Virginia Bradford had become a star of the silent movies and married money, the Estes, as with so many Southern families impoverished by what they called the War of Northern Aggression, had been aristocratic but dirt poor. Virginia, too, was cosmopolitan in her way. She lived for a time in London and one of her four husbands was the triple agent Cedric Belfrage, who spied for the Americans the British and the Soviets.

Realising that with his slight stammer he had no real future in the movies, Bill, energetic and multi-talented, bought cheap desert land

Gavin Maxwell: sleeping author and sleeping otter, early 1960s

near Hollywood, designed and built high-end houses and sold them at a handsome profit. His ceramics were eagerly taken up by the boutiques and when he needed a break he enrolled in UCLA and took a degree in music. He continued to be based in Hollywood, but on his frequent visits to the United Kingdom he would call in on Val and me in the North on his journeys between Scotland and his apartment in Notting Hill, where he kept all his portable possessions piled on the grand piano to deter a clever and inquisitive otter who liked to dismantle everything.

199

Bill's hand-painted 1982 Christmas card showing Phoebe at Camusfearna
William Estes Lyons

Bill's mother Virginia lived to be ninety-six years old. Her lifelong friend and companion was a feisty black lady of similar vintage and they fought like cat and cat. According to Bill's Tennessee cousin Bobby Mann, this was a fairly common exchange:

'Miss Virginia, y'all oughtta treat me with more respect!'

'Respect yuh? We used to *own* four hundred of yuh.'

This, Bobby told us, was an exaggeration typical of the Confederate branch of the family: 'Virginia's and Billy's heads are full of notions of a South they never knew. Billy served in the US Navy from 1942 to 1945 but when he refers to "The War" it's not *that* one he's thinking of.'

Bobby Mann, sixty years old, courtly and immaculate in white linen suit, broad-brimmed panama and polka-dot silk tie, was the image of the Southern gentleman but he did not share his cousin's romantic notions. Bill had told us with patent sincerity: 'When I was a child I had some negro friends. They used to come round to the back door until it finally occurred to them that they were welcome to come to the front.' Bobby, while agreeing that race relations were better than they had been in his youth, said they had never been as easy as that and even 120 years after emancipation he felt that the most one could hope for was a wary mutual tolerance.

'There are a few white men who marry blacks,' conceded Bobby, and added with an unconscious racism that took our breath away, 'but for me those negro ladies just look too like animals.'

We were visiting Bobby at his home in Memphis during our meandering four-thousand-mile drive from New England to El Salvador in Central America. The year was 1991. George Bush senior was in the White House and his vice president, Dan Quayle, was notorious for his frequent linguistic faux pas, such as assuring an elementary school class that 'potato' was spelt P-O-T-A-T-O-E. The media had given Quayle a rough ride, but Bobby was inclined to allow him the benefit of the doubt. 'I did not believe that the Vice President of the United States of America could be so much of a fool as he was being portrayed, so when I read in the paper that Senator Quayle was due to make a speech in Memphis I decided to go along and see for myself.'

'And...' I queried.

'He's an idiot,' said Bobby sadly.

I remembered this conversation a couple of months later when I met Pete at a US Embassy garden party in San Salvador. Pete worked for USAID, which was doing reconstruction work in that war-lacerated little country. A former American football player, his high, spluttering voice was completely incongruent with his towering refrigerator-like physique. If you can imagine parrot-face comedian Freddy Davies with a strong Bronx accent, you'll have a rough idea of how he sounded. Pete didn't hesitate to flutter in where seraphim might have feared to fly.

'So you're from England,' he spluttered, 'that backward little island that still has a monarchy. Isn't it time you people got real and got rid of all that nonsense. In any case, I really do think your Queen Elizabeth is a complete pill. Don't you agree?'

It took me a moment to recover from this summary assessment of my Head of State by a man I'd met only sixty seconds earlier, but I replied, 'Well no, Pete, I believe Her Maj does a demanding job with dignity and devotion. And when I remember that you Yanks actually *elected* Dan Quayle as your VP I'm more than satisfied with our backward little island.'

'Oh! Now you're just being offensive.'

Pete's scathing dismissal of the Supreme Governor of the Church of England, Head of the Commonwealth of Nations and Queen of sixteen of its fifty-three member states, was untypical of the majority of his compatriots, many of whom are actively enthusiastic about our monarchy, though on my earliest visits to the United States it took me a while to cotton on to the informal manner in which this feeling was sometimes expressed.

'How *is* Elizabeth?' a blue-rinsed matron quizzed me before a commencement luncheon at our twin school in Massachusetts.

'Elizabeth? Oh, you mean the Queen. She's fine. At least, I assume she is. We're not on really intimate terms, you understand.'

'So you haven't actually met her?'

'Not to gossip with, though we did once share a cathedral... with a thousand or so other folk, that is.'

'Oh, I must say, I find that rather disappointing, especially as you come from London.'

'I don't, as it happens, and even if I did, London's a big place.'

'Really? But England's such a little country.'

'True, but there are well over eight million people in the capital. Slightly more than in New York, as a matter of fact.'

American insularity still exists but it's not as marked as it used to be. No doubt the change began in the two world wars, but exponentially improving communications have also played an enormous role. Since 1890, four generations of my own family, including one of my sons, have emigrated to the United States. Initially the divided clan did its best to keep in touch, first by letter and later, in better-off days, by exchanging widely-spaced transatlantic visits. Then cheap flights and Ancestry.com changed everything. Not long ago I stood in a Michigan living room with my first cousin several times removed, and gazed at a photo of my fourteen-year-old future mother proudly holding a swimming trophy won in Wigan in 1933. My son Richard plays bass in a rock band in Minneapolis with his fourth generation cousin Paul, while their little

European Otter   *David Rentoul/ Shutterstock*

blonde daughters, as uncannily alike as popcorns, tackle the swings and climbing frame in a nearby park.

Unfortunately my own parents carelessly forgot to provide me with a sister, so I had to make do with Shirley Temple and Judy Garland, who were readily available because at least four out of every five films shown in our local flea-pit seemed to have come from the USA. It was something of a one-way traffic and I somehow doubt that Elizabeth Larner and Stanley Holloway were as celebrated in Poughkeepsie as John Wayne and Roger Rogers were in Wigan. But in the past twenty years or more a revolution has occurred. Americans enthuse about

British films and TV shows and it's not just *Downton* and *Harry Potter*. A couple of years ago, Val and I discovered a huge, rambling and delightfully chaotic antique shop in the little Minnesota town of Jordan. Having partially explored this warren I sidled up to the desk and said hesitantly to the owner, 'Have you ever by any chance seen a British TV show called *The Last of the Summer Wine*?'

She smiled broadly. 'Yes indeed, this place is exactly like Aunty Wainwright's, isn't it?'

So we are no longer quite so divided by a common language, but the idea that we Brits all live within a hoot and a holler of Horse Guards Parade is still deeply ingrained in the psyche of some Americans. That first conversation with Bill Lyons, always of course vastly less insular than I could ever be, took place more than forty years ago and since then I have been a frequent visitor to the USA. I land at O'Hare or Logan or JFK and introduce myself to the local representatives of Alamo, that worldwide brotherhood of Texan patriots. The friendly clerk summons up a printout of my rental booking, and I have lost count of the number of times my address appears as 'London, England'. It isn't a big deal, of course, but, on one occasion only, I decided, like Davy Crocket and company, to make a stand.

'I don't live anywhere near London. I live in Wigan. That's two hundred miles from London.'

'So it's in the same neighbourhood, right?'

'Wrong. I know two hundred miles is just a step to McDonald's for you Americans, but in our small island we think it's a considerable journey.'

'No problem. Just dictate your full address to me and I'll type it into the contract.'

It was only some days later that I looked at the printout and saw that it read:

John Sharrock Taylor
Billinge Road
Pemberton
Wigan
LONDON
England.

Eden Was In Appley Bridge

The problem with Moses was that, being from Yorkshire, he didn't know his atlas from his A-to-Z. A land flowing with milk and honey was what the Lord had promised the Israelites when they escaped from slavery in Egypt, but Moses never even got to enter Canaan, and there are several conflicting theories about that. The Bible tells us it was because he grabbed all the credit for finding water in a dry place, when he should really have given thanks to God, but there's an old song that gives an alternative explanation:

> *Moses was a prophet*
> *Of good West Riding stock.*
> *He brought forth some water*
> *By striking on a rock.*
> *The Israelites all gathered round*
> *And gave a mighty cheer*
> *But weren't they disappointed*
> *When they found it wasn't beer!*

In fact both these theories are wrong. The real reason for Moses's exclusion from Canaan was geographical. It's only 265 miles from Cairo to Jerusalem. That's less than a day's drive in a Land Rover and even my Aunt Maud could have biked it in a fortnight, but either the old boy *had* discovered an oasis with an inexhaustible spring of Sam Smith's, or his TomTom was on the blink, because the Israelites wandered round the desert for all of forty years before finally reaching their new home.

Even setting aside his dysfunctional grasp of geography, Moses was never much of a popular success as a prophet. To begin with, there was all that 'Thou-Shalt-Not' and 'Keep-Taking-the-Tablets' stuff. Then there was the directive against golden calves (when any red-blooded Israelite male, stuck in the middle of a desert, would have died for a glimpse of a well-filled stocking). Finally, as a Jewish friend once explained to me, there was that disgraceful business of crossing the Red Sea.

'Disgraceful?' I asked, puzzled.

'Certainly. If Moses had only had the sense to turn left instead of showing off with the conjuring tricks, *we'd* have had the oil instead of leaving it for the Arabs.'

And when the Israelites did at last reach their destination, they found that the Promised Land was by no means all it had been cracked up to be. For a start, it was not just occupied, but jam-packed, shoulder-to-shoulder, standing room only, with Canaanites, Hittites, Jebusites, Amorites, Girgashites, Hivites, Arkites, Sinites, Arvadites, Zemarites, Hamathites, Sodomites, Simmonites, Bauxites, Haematites, Trilobites, Ammonites, Stalagmites and Marmites. These established locals were naturally less than happy to welcome yet another motley gang of interlopers, and the Israelites' entrance marked the very beginning of what we now know as the Middle-East Problem. Indeed, a ruckus immediately kicked off which has gone on for the past three-and-a-quarter millennia, making the Hundred Years War look like a playground scuffle. And, as if that wasn't enough, there was the really awful Palestinian plumbing to contend with. 'Moab was my wash-pot and over Edom did I cast out my shoe,' muttered King David bitterly, proving that even in the royal palace there wasn't such a thing as a viable shower or a bidet that didn't leak.

The truth of the matter is that *every* silver lining has its cloud and every garden its snake in the grass. And this (whisper it not in Gathurst, tell it not in the streets of Aspull) even applies to that most-nearly-perfect of all terrestrial paradises, God's Own Country, the County Palatine (a term derived of course from 'Palestine') of Lancaster.

It has long been understood that Biblical history began in Mesopotamia, the Land Between the Rivers, but the major mistake of the anthropologists has been their erroneous assumption that the rivers in question were the Tigris and the Euphrates, whereas, after intensive research, I can now reveal that the garden where Eve tempted Adam with the forbidden fruit was located, appropriately enough, in the hamlet of Appley Bridge, just outside the County Borough of Wigan, well to the south of Morecambe Bay and slightly to the west of Mount Ararat (now known as Rivington Pike), a land laved by the limpid waters of the Ribble and the Mersey and guarded in the north from the Cumbrian barbarians by a stream which is known to this very day as the River Eden.

Now, I realise that there exist certain benighted folk, who, permanently mortified by the humiliating misfortune of having been born on the wrong side of the Pennines, may dispute my county's claim to be the cradle of civilization, but just murmur the ancient Hebrew mantra: 'tripe, cow-heels, cockles, black puddings, jam butties, parkin, Eccles cakes, rugby league, clogs and cricket' and the case is proved. It is written 'stay me with flagons; comfort me with apples', but was it not the Wigan patriarch Uncle Joseph who fed the people, not with manna, but with Mint Balls? Did not our Warriors rout Sentellins with only the jawbone of a tyke, and didn't the mighty Statham skittle all the Amalekites for nobbut a savoury duck?

The great Westhoughton poet John Donne wrote that his personal paradise was tainted by 'the serpent love that can convert manna into gall', and it is sad to record that even the County Palatine has a single, solitary drawback. Why did the prophet Arkwright decree that the twelve tribes of our ancestors should not, like Bradford's Philistines, array themselves in robes of wool? The answer is that Lancashire is very damp, and very damp is very good for cotton. But very damp is also very good, or rather very bad, for a much less pleasing fluid than Canaan's milk and honey, which is why Manchester's speech is flatter than its caps and Liverpudlians talk with an accent ten per cent Irish and ninety per cent catarrh. Why do we Lancastrians have the reputation of being phlegmatic? The term comes from 'phlegm', which was the cold and moist one of the four humours of Platonic philosophy. So annoy any one of us and you may get a snotty answer. It's why, in addition to Halle's Band, *Coronation Street*, the Verve, George Formby and Beecham's pills, Lancashire provided the world with Thermogene and Fisherman's Friends. And it's also why I sojourn here in sunny Spain and write my monthly article for *The Andalucian* rather than the *Wigan Ob*.

CHAPTER 17

TURNED OUT NICE AGAIN

Little George Booth's daddy was the man who gave Wigan the Pier, and even if he had not been such a towering talent he would be remembered for that alone. George's dad was a comedian, a great one, but he didn't want his lad to follow him on to the stage, so young George became a jockey. But the boy was no Gordon Richards, and after riding forty-two horses into second place he decided that it wasn't for him. George's father had died in 1921 as a result of the post-war influenza pandemic, but George's mother had kept all his costumes and props, so George thought he would try to re-create some of his dad's music hall routines. He knew very well that the old man's shoes were too big for him, so he adopted his mother's maiden name and billed himself as George Hoy. Many years later he told Roy Plomley, 'If I was going to flop, I didn't want to drag my dad's name into it.' He showed the same humility when he contemplated his own death. As is right and proper, the inscriptions on the family grave in Warrington Cemetery give pride of place to George Senior, and George Junior is a footnote:

ALSO GEORGE FORMBY OBE
SON OF THE ABOVE WHO DIED ON 6TH MARCH 1961
AGED 56 YEARS

That funeral was the biggest send-off in British show business history. The cortege wound its way through streets lined with 150,000 mourners who had come to pay homage to one of the country's best-loved entertainers. That was well over half a century ago but the fiftieth anniversary generated a rash of journalistic comment, much of it patronising. God save the creators from the critics. There is a hoary old saying in the theatrical world that the hacks who write the reviews are like the eunuchs in the harem. They know exactly how it should be done. They see it done every night, but when it comes to doing it themselves… well, you know the rest. Celebrity death anniversaries are

George Formby

the breath of life to the scribblers because they provide such a splendid opportunity to clog-dance on famous graves, and the anniversary of 2011 brought out the hoofers in force. Formby's success, they chorused, was inexplicable. He had little or no talent. He couldn't sing. He couldn't act. He couldn't even read music. Well, chaps, I have news for you, neither could the Beatles, Lionel Bart or many who starred at La Scala and Covent Garden.

Several of these self-styled experts took George to task for his simplistic strumming on the ukulele and here, chaps, brace yourselves for more news. The instrument on which George made his name wasn't the ukulele at all. It didn't sound like the ukulele. It didn't even look like the ukulele. Combining a ukulele finger-board with a banjo body, the ukulele-banjo, or banjolele, is a much more sophisticated instrument with a bigger tonal range than the simple uke. And as for the strumming, Formby played in a range of complex rhythmic idioms, including the triple, the fan, the shake and, especially, the split-stroke which was his trademark style. A throwaway piece of facetiousness by George himself in a TV interview was responsible for another piece of misinformation much repeated by the hacks: In his stage act Formby used several instruments tuned to different pitches and he told the interviewer, tongue in cheek, that this was because he could only play in one key.

Talent is hard to pin down in words but easy to recognise when you see it in action. George Formby was one of the first stars to entertain the troops in World War Two, as was the delightful Joyce Grenfell, who remarked to her accompanist, 'Well, I don't quite know what he's got, but whatever it is, he's certainly got it. He has them eating out of his hand.' That was in the North African desert. George took one look at it and said 'Ee, It's just like Blackpool sands!' and the audience of 10,000 soldiers was with him before he had even played a note. Less than ten years later he walked on stage at the Royal Alexander Theatre, Toronto, peered into the packed audience, recognised an old Lancashire mate and said 'Ee, Walter, is that really you?' They dined together after the show and no doubt Walter dined out on the incident for the rest of his life.

George had millions of fans from all walks of life, from dustmen to the Royal Family, and by the late 1930s he was making more than

£100,000 a year from films, records and stage appearances. His £500,000 contract with Columbia Pictures (£18,000,000 in today's money) made him the world's fifth-biggest star, ahead of Errol Flynn, Bette Davis and even Bing Crosby. As with Norman Wisdom and Charlie Chaplin (who copied that silly walk from George's dad) the secret of Formby's attraction lay in a vulnerable, anarchic, endearing character who played on the British love of the underdog. George was an oddity, an outsider, a genuine original. Dame Thora Hird said simply: 'He was sent by God.'

And he really could sing. He wasn't a Sinatra, of course, that wasn't his style, but those deft, witty, pattering lyrics were part of a tradition that started with early music hall, went on through Gilbert and Sullivan and the Two Ronnies, and still continues with the rappers of today. George's romantic record 'Leaning on a Lamp-Post' sold 150,000 copies within a month of its release in 1937, but he could switch in a flash to the seaside-postcard sauciness of 'With my Little Stick of Blackpool Rock', which he sang with a wide-eyed goofy innocence that disarmed the suggestiveness of the lyric. Not everyone was enamoured. George Orwell thought his namesake's act was 'low' and straight-laced Aunty BBC unwittingly promoted the record sales of Formby's naughtier songs by banning them from the air.

George Formby had talent all right, but he couldn't have done any of it without his missus, and if George, living or dead, continues to be an Aunt Sally for the scribbling fraternity, Beryl is their prime choice for the Wicked Witch of West Lancs. What attracted the pretty blonde dancer to the hesitant, gormless fledgling comedian from Wigan? It must have been his raw talent, because most folk who knew them reckoned she didn't actually fancy him, though the claws were rapidly unsheathed if any other lass even smiled in his direction. Betty Driver and Irene Handl were both clawed. Pat Kirkwood, his glamorous co-star, described George as 'cretinous… if you tried to converse with him, you'd find there was no one at home' but she'd got hold of the wrong end of the clapper-board. George wasn't stupid, just terrified at the idea of Beryl catching him talking to another woman.

Beryl took one look at George and knew she could turn him into a star. It was she who got him to take up that signature banjolele, she who won him his first recording contract with Edison-Bell. When she insisted on being on set at rehearsals the judgemental journos put it down to jealousy and control-freakery, but the fact is that she had to be there. George may not have been illiterate in the strictest sense of the word, but there is no way he could have coped with an entire film script without her help. As it was, Beryl coached him through each movie, scene by scene, line by line. During live performances she stood in the wings with a clipboard and a stopwatch impatiently monitoring every moment of George's act, more like an ambitious showbiz mother than a wife.

Beryl was no respecter of persons. It didn't matter if you were Lord Reith the Director General of the BBC or Uncle Joe himself, if Beryl had you in her sights you got it between the eyes. The film director Monty Banks said of her: 'The only time you'll get me shooting anything with that fucking Formby woman will be when she is playing the murder victim and the scene is for real.' The South African apartheid politician Daniel Malan would have agreed. When he berated her for kissing a little black girl who had presented her with a bouquet she put him firmly in his place: 'Why don't you piss off, you horrible little man?'

The truth is that George-and-Beryl was a double act, rather like George-and-Mildred and even more like George-and-the-Dragon. George loved to be loved and in fact his being loved was essential to the public persona Beryl had built up for him. She was the one who negotiated with impresarios and dealt with troublesome cast members. Knowing his taste for booze and chorus girls, she kept tight control of the finances, which gave him a wonderful excuse for never buying a round of drinks: 'Beryl only lets me have five bob a week pocket money, y'know.' She spelled their relationship out in a press interview. 'I think a comedian shouldn't have business worries and George likes to feel carefree. He hasn't had a row with anyone in show business. I do all the battling. I don't care what they say about me; I *do* care what they say about George.'

They lived in style. Their yacht was the *Lady Beryl*. The stone-mullioned residence on the front at Lytham St Anne's was the last of a series of increasingly opulent houses all called *Beryldene*. But though they enjoyed the trappings that came with celebrity some things were more important than money, and they turned down a lucrative twenty-week tour of Australia because they were worried about the health of

Willie Waterbucket, their fifteen-year-old dog.

So much contradictory stuff has been written about that marriage that the truth remains elusive. And in any case, who can ever truthfully say that they fully understand that most intimate of relationships from the outside, or even, I sometimes think, from the inside? In a press interview after her death, George is famously quoted as saying 'My life with Beryl was hell'. Frankly, I don't believe it was, or at least not all of it. The fact is that Beryl transformed George from a kid into a star and it came at the price of the savage discipline she exacted. But somewhere behind the glittering stardust the kid was still there, and kids can be both thoughtless and ruthless when they feel the leading reins slacken. Beryl died from leukaemia on Christmas Day 1960. The last months had been a torment for both of them, as she raged against fate and washed down the morphine with ever more alcohol. There were dreadful scenes on set, and George muttered to Tommy Trinder that he and Beryl were finished. Trinder said later, 'It was like a blind man saying he was going to get rid of his guide dog.'

But with Beryl dead and buried, school was finally out for boy George. Two months after his wife's death he announced his engagement to teacher Pat Howson, twenty years his junior. It was not to be. A forty-a-day man, whose favourite snack was beef-dripping toast, George pulled out of his Christmas pantomime with a heavy cold which soon turned to pneumonia and on 6 March 1961, just two days before his planned wedding to Pat, he died of heart failure. He had survived Beryl by just fourteen months.

Harried by Beryl's indomitable spirit, George had made it big. Very big. Bigger even than his dad, though he wouldn't have thanked you for saying so. He still has thousands, if not millions, of fans, though there are also the knockers and nay-sayers, even in Wigan. When Amanda Barton's splendid bronze statue was erected in 2007 they ensured that it was shoved down a dead-end where nobody would see it. I'm glad to report that it has finally been moved into the light of day, so I suppose one could say that it's turned out nice again for Wigan's most famous son. I suppose a statue of battling Beryl would be too much to hope for?

New Year With Machine Gun And Tank

Velvety dusk in a tropical garden blazing with red poinsettias and cascading with purple bougainvillea. We stand on our friends' terrace sipping Pilsner beer with the lights of San Salvador gleaming far below. The first distant detonations begin to roll across the valley: the sharp, high-pitched volleys of jack-jumpers and the deep-throated roar of bangers. And what bangers! Forget the puny productions of Brock and Standard. A Salvadoran banger consists of a *Prensa Gráfica* Sunday newspaper rolled into a thick-walled three-inch diameter tube and stuffed with gunpowder. One of these monsters, half-buried in the vacant lot across the street, has just hurled half a hundredweight of earth and gravel against the bathroom window.

Smoke billows across the scene and the city lights twinkle through it like sparklers. In a garden on the hill opposite ours, a wilder party is in full swing. Drums pulse and shadowy figures gyrate against the glare of Roman candles. We wonder if they will eventually notice that they have set their garage on fire. Rockets ascend from the Estadio Nacional in multi-coloured starbursts above the vibrating city.

By midnight the individual detonations have melded into a continuous roar. A Somme offensive must have sounded something like this. And, as if to complement my thought, a steep, intermittent parabola of green light sprouts from below. Somebody is firing tracer from a machine gun.

Arriving back home about one o'clock on New Year's morning, I was unable to swing the van into the car port because the gateway was blocked by a camouflage-painted armoured car which looked very like Lieutenant Grüber's little tank in *Allo! Allo!* Entering by the pedestrian gate, we were startled by a movement in the darkness. A patrol of eight soldiers in battle fatigues was seated on our garage floor clutching automatic rifles and looking both nervous and sheepish. Not one of

them looked to be more than sixteen and I remembered that Salvadoran soldiers were often forcibly recruited from their school desks. Feeling slightly ridiculous I said to their NCO, 'Sargento, I'm tired and I want to put my car away. Kindly move your tank. And anyway, what are you doing in my garage?'

The young man apologised profusely. It seemed that their post ought to have been outside the supermarket at the bottom of the street but a previous patrol had recently been sprayed with machine gun fire from a passing truck and several of them killed.

'Sir, the fact is, we're scared.'

'I'm not surprised. OK, stay put, but I don't expect to see you or your tank when I look out of my window in the morning. Happy New Year.'

'Feliz año, señor, y muchisimas gracias.'

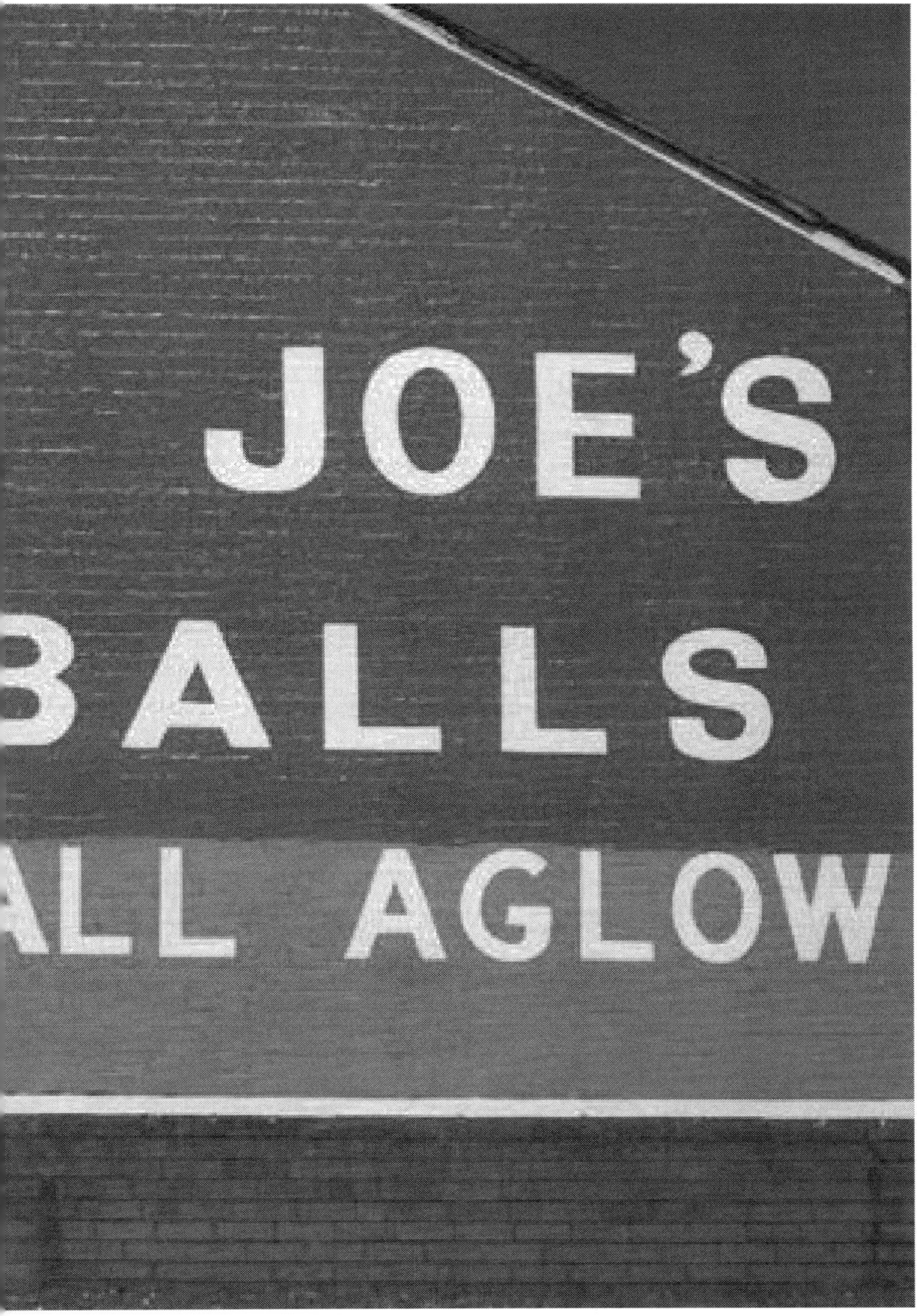
JOE'S
BALLS
ALL AGLOW

ACKNOWLEDGEMENTS

When 'Omer smote 'is bloomin' lyre,
  He'd 'eard men sing by land an' sea;
An' what he thought 'e might require,
  'E went an' took – the same as me!

From Rudyard Kipling's Introduction to the *Barrack-Room Ballads*

I don't know one end of a rugby ball from the other (What? Surely you don't mean to tell me they're both the same?), so my brother Stephen Taylor has supplied all of the sensible stuff in the chapter *Up for th' Cup*.

Avril Fishwick, sometime High Sheriff of Greater Manchester and daughter of the eponymous buccaneer in *The Pedant and the Pirate*, told me much of that story and was also one of the two *Bletchley girls*. Since I finished writing *Six Steps*, Avril has left us, full of years and honours, as has my dear friend David Cutter, for many years director of music at Wigan Parish Church.

My wife Val and her sister Margaret grew up with half of the tale of *Winnie and Wilson* which sounds as if it could have come straight out of an Arnold Bennett novel. It was while trawling the Internet that I discovered the surprising connection with the 1950s civil rights movement in the Deep South of the USA.

Les Soucis de Quasimodo is the kind of shaggy dog story I used to tell my first-form students. Like all folk tales it started small and grew to its present length over years of embroidery. *Getting it Right* is the kind of story I *didn't* use to tell my first-form students, as is *A Load of Muck and an Actor*, which has its origins in a tale told by Ronnie Cunliffe, Head Verger and jobbing actor, in the Bridge Inn after a cathedral choir rehearsal one Friday evening in Newcastle-upon-Tyne. *Laughing Roundhead*, an anecdote for all seasons, was part of the survival kit of my Lancaster University debating partner Ken Todd, who had a fund of such yarns for those frequent occasions when we couldn't think of anything remotely sensible to say about whatever serious topic was under discussion.

About a fifth of the book has appeared previously in one form or another, either in my monthly column in *The Andalucian* magazine or in one of my previously published books. *In the Beginning was the Nerd* and *Carols in Delhi* are from *No Baboons in India*. *Christmas in Hospital* and *Christmas Eve in Wigan* (including a sharply observed carol parody by that doyen of Wigan journalists John Benn) first appeared in my early years autobiography *A Wigan Childhood*, as did part of *Mining Butty*. Other material for that story came from John Burnett's book *Useful Toil*. John Vose's *The Lancashire Caruso* was a helpful source for my chapter of the same name as was Linda Esther Gray's *A Life on the High Cs* for my *Eva the Diva*.

Geoffrey Bond's book *Lakonia* and Geoffrey Marchbanks' *The Painted Ship* were sources for my account of the *Lakonia* disaster as were several Internet sites such as Rick Spilman's *Old Salt Blog* and *Andalucia.com* which, at the time of the 50th Anniversary commemoration in 2013, extensively quoted Gordon Holme's first-hand reminiscences of the rescue operation.

Finally, special thanks to Uncle Joe and the Directors of William Santus & Co Ltd of Wigan for keeping us all aglow for so many years and for generously allowing me to use their logo.

John Sharrock Taylor
El Cortijo del Rector
In the hills of Andalusia
August 2016

Printed in Great Britain
by Amazon